Learn the Secret
Language of Dreams

Pamela Cummins

Cover Design by Brent Meske

ISBN-10: 0-9976703-0-4
ISBN-13: 978-0-9976703-0-1

To the Dreamer in You

Contents

Foreword

What an honor it is to have been asked to write the Foreword for Pamela Cummins' book *Learn the Secret Language of Dreams.* Dream interpretation has always been a favorite topic of mine, because, well, who doesn't dream, right? It makes for great conversation while trying to figure out the meaning of a dream.

I first met Pamela Cummins when I began putting together my free online magazine, *Bellesprit*, a spiritually based magazine that would share knowledge freely for those interested in learning more about the metaphysical world. Pamela joined the magazine writing *The Love Channel*, a column answering questions about relationships. With her unique guidance, often featuring song lyrics, her column quickly became a hit with our readers.

Within a few months, Pamela also inherited our dream interpretation column called, *In the Dreamtime.* Each month our readers would submit their interesting or strange dreams awaiting Pamela's quick wit and intuitive knowledge around the message their dream had to share. I became intrigued - as did our readers - with Pamela's ability to read into a dream and find within the message the Universe had for the dreamer. It's truly fascinating to follow her column and see how she came up with such incredible guidance found within the secret language of our dreams.

In my own career as a Psychic, Medium and Instructor, my personal work with dreams has always been astonishing. When we go to sleep at night, our soul travels to other realms where we are taught lessons, heal the broken, or assist others. During this time, this is where we find ourselves in the fascinating world of dreams. We are shown the problems we are facing, how they are affecting us, and then how to solve that problem. It's about learning how to look for the symbols found within the dream to piece the puzzle together. Pamela does an amazing job of making this task easy to understand and spells out how you, too, can interpret your own dreams.

As you read this book, you will see what I mean. You'll be scratching your head at some of the interpretations, wondering how you can do this, too. I promise you, if you read this book in its entirety and follow the steps recommended you will be able to understand the secret language of your own dreams and discover the messages the Universe has for you.

Life is easy, we just make it hard. Look for the signs, they're there to guide us along our journey.

Belle Salisbury is the owner and creator of Bellesprit Magazine found online at www.bellesprit.com. She is a well-known psychic medium and instructor of metaphysics, including Psychic Development and Mediumship. You can learn more about Belle at www.bellesalisbury.com.

Introduction

The journey of learning and understanding your personal dream symbolism is a lifelong process; you must be willing to dedicate the time to write down your dreams, observe recurring symbols, and look within to see the truth of where you are in your current life. Many people seem daunted by this prospect because we live in an instant gratification world. They want to know why they dreamed of swimming in a cesspool or being chased by someone, so they think the answer lies in a dream dictionary. These types of dream books are a good start, yet one symbol could have many meanings, and when you mix in each individual with their different life stories, one symbol has endless interpretations. You will learn more about this in Chapter One regarding dream symbolism.

This book, *Learn the Secret Language of Dreams,* will introduce you to the different styles of dreams that occur in the dreamtime to aid you in understanding what the dream language is all about. You may be asking yourself, "Why should I bother spending my time learning the mystery of my dreams?" The reason is there is no denial in the dreamtime, only subconscious and spiritual truths. While you are dreaming your dreams, you receive answers to your problems, warnings about possible health issues, what your heart truly desires, and other secrets that are locked within you. Wouldn't you like to discover answers to these and much more?

The different styles of dreaming this book covers are environment dreams, recurring dreams, solution dreams, body and health dreams, departed loved ones who visit in your dreams, precognitive dreams, nightmares, and spiritual dreams. There is also a chapter on love and relationship dreams because this is another passion I specialize in. This book does *not* include lucid dreaming (when you are aware that you're dreaming) as this style is not the author's expertise. Another type of dream style that is not my specialty is post-traumatic stress disorder dreams; in fact, I will only work with a client who is in therapy with a psychotherapist for these dreams. If you are having these types of dreams, please know it is impossible to recover alone, and to seek a professional to help you through the healing of post-traumatic stress disorder in order to recover and thrive.

Now you might be thinking, "Who is this woman and what makes her a dream expert?" I have been graced with the ability to remember my dreams and the earliest dream I can recall is at the age of six when a witch was chasing my childhood crush and myself. I used to laugh about how silly my dreams were, just like the majority of the population, and I was unaware of the secret treasures my dreams held. That all changed in 1989 when I began my personal growth and spiritual path. I knew intuitively that I needed to resolve my childhood issues for the sake of moving forward to a more fulfilling and positive life. I went to therapy and a few different types of twelve step programs, which helped to trigger dreams that I knew were repressed memories. I asked God to please send me a good therapist, and my prayers were answered with an awesome one. My therapist specialized in dream interpretation and for several years she helped me understand my dreams in our weekly sessions. I started having precognitive dreams which went against my therapist's belief system. This started to cause problems in our sessions. Then my health insurance started hassling me about the type of therapy I was receiving. I took this as a sign to move on. Eventually, I started having fewer precognitive dreams as my psychic abilities (that I had shut off in my childhood) returned to my waking life. I continued to record my dreams for another eight years in order to go deeper into my personal dream language. I also read many books on dream interpretation and quickly learned that dream dictionaries were too basic for my dreams. After a while, my friends and family would come to me with their dreams, and it was inevitable that I included dream analysis in my practice. I have had the honor of doing interpretation on my and other's radio shows and writing for Bellesprit Magazine as their dream expert since February of 2013.

The majority of the dreams and interpretations in the following chapters are from the readers of my *In the Dreamtime* monthly column in Bellesprit Magazine www.bellesprit.com/author/LoveChannel and several clients gave me permission to use their dreams. All names have been changed to protect their identity. I also used my own dreams because obviously it is much easier for me to remember their details. I used these dreams as examples to help you understand each type of dream style much more clearly.

Many people will tell me that they do not remember their dreams so how could they possibly interpret them? Fortunately, the process of remembering your dreams is a lot simpler than learning how to do dream interpretation. You can get the free gift *How to Remember Your Dreams* with a guide and meditation at www.learndreaminterpretation.com.

I highly recommend that you record your dreams in a journal, laptop, tablet, mobile phone, or a voice recording device. You may think that you will remember your dreams; however, the reality is that your memories of the dream will fade away as you go about your day. When you record your dreams you have a reference that you can go back to again and again to help you learn your dream language. Time constraints and duties may prevent you from recording your entire dream, instead, record the highlights and feelings. A few of my clients draw their dreams, write a poem, or make up a song lyric; do what feels right for you.

Are you ready to begin your journey into the secret language of dreams? Turn the page...

Chapter One

Dream Symbolism

Would you like to understand your dream symbolism? Some people have a dream, go to a dream dictionary, look up a symbol, and think that is what their dream means. The dream language is more complicated than that and takes many years to learn. Dream dictionaries, books on general symbolism, the different types of angels, Gods, Goddess, and animal totems are very helpful to start to understand basic symbols. One book that really helped me at the beginning of my journey was *The Secret Language of Signs* by Denise Linn.

What really assisted me to understand different symbols was learning tarot, because the tarot cards instruction book's meaning of a certain card can be something different depending on what cards are placed next to it. A wise woman told me to sleep with my deck. I did, which helped me learn it faster, and produced some really interesting dreams.

I often tell my clients and readers of my dream column

that you are your best interpreter of your dreams. Nevertheless, it takes years to understand the complexity of your own symbolism. Some symbols make perfect sense, yet others are quite baffling. The different dreams styles add even more of a twist into comprehending your dream signs. When you mix in what is going on in your life, it could make interpreting your dreams even more interesting and/or complicated. Can you understand why a dream dictionary can be compared to a first grader's textbook?

Let's use the cat as an example of how one thing can have many different meanings. If you look up the meaning of cat in a symbol book or on the internet, you would find the following: intuition, mysterious, independent, luxury, and feminine. A kitty's purr would be associated with healing or pleasure. The meaning of a black cat could be seen as bad luck. You can see how a feline can mean many different things.

In a cat lover's dream the feline would bring a feeling of love and companionship. They could have a dream that predicts a new kitty will be their pet in the future. In Chapter Seven you will read about how my cat, Midnite, visited me after her death in my dream. A kitty that is hissing may be a nightmare for someone who is afraid of cats. Yet for someone else who is having issues with a girlfriend, the hissing cat could stand for the friend being catty.

My hope for using the cat example is to get you to understand that learning the message of the nighttime is much more complex in comparison to learning to speak a foreign language. I want to be fair, so now it is time to cater to dog lovers. The next excerpt is from one of my columns in *Bellesprit Magazine* regarding the symbolism of dogs in dreams.

Dog Dreams

Dogs are very loyal and very protective of their masters. Dogs also have unconditional love for their owners and put up with being mistreated. In this context, dreaming of a dog could mean that you need to be more loving towards someone. Or to protect yourself and not to allow yourself to be abused. It could also mean that you need to be more loyal to someone. Perhaps, someone is very loyal and protective of you. It really all depends upon all the other symbolism and feelings of the dreamer to get a proper interpretation.

Talking about feelings, if you are a dog lover, when you dream about dogs, the feeling usually is one of love and happiness. You feel part of the "pack" with dogs. Although, if you are scared of dogs or don't like dogs, even a friendly one will make a dream unpleasant.

LOL, I keep hearing the song, "Who Let the Dogs Out." In some cases the dog could symbolize a man who is very sexual and inappropriate about it. The majority of people have seen a male dog who is humping something he shouldn't! Not to say this couldn't be symbolic for a female.

Lastly, if you dream of a ferocious dog, that is a symbolism of danger. If the dog is locked up, that could be someone or something that is threatening, but it is contained. It could also be a part of you that is dangerous. When you dream of a dog chasing you or even attacking you, that is telling you there is someone or something in your life that is not safe. Please pay attention to what that could be and protect yourself in your waking hours.

Till the next dreamtime, may all your dreams be sweet!

The next dream was very easy for me to interpret because I have been doing it for decades. The person who submitted this dream to the column did not feel that it was so easy.

Baby Items Dream

I woke up early this morning so angry with my hubby... lol. In the dream, I was sitting in the driver's seat of our vehicle, my husband was sitting alongside of me. We seemed to be looking for a receipt for something and I said, "Here it is," picking up a rather long receipt from the floor board. When I looked at the receipt I was shocked at what it said. The first thing I noticed was a purchase of a baby walker, and the next was the total of the receipt, $188. The entire receipt was a list for baby items my husband had purchased. When I questioned him as to why he was buying baby items, he replied, "I have a baby!"

Dream Interpretation

I love the symbolism in your dream because it is so straight forward to me. The fact that you were in the driver's seat is saying you are in control of your life and are the boss in this marriage (don't tell your husband). The good news is that he is also your equal because he is sitting in the front passenger seat, as opposed to the back seat.

The receipt to me is a symbol of things in your marriage. The fact that you are looking at it together is a good thing. The baby items are most likely a symbol of something new, not a child. The new could be some new things coming in your marriage. However, the fact that it was your husband's receipt for items that he purchased – the new could be a new project that he is working on. Or another meaning could be you are angry about some of his recent purchases and/or the way he spends money.

The amount also has meaning. Does the number 188 mean anything to you? I took a quick look at two different websites where it meant success and money flow. If you add the numbers together in numerology it comes to 8, which is interesting because there are two 8's in the number. When I looked at three other websites they said the number 8 is about wealth, abundance and balance. This is very interesting because of the fact that these numbers were on a money receipt. Lastly, I am intuitively getting that in order to receive money, you and your husband need to spend money.

Amazing Symbolism Dream

My friend, Lisa, mentioned to me that she was totally baffled and grossed out upon reading this next dream in the magazine. I blushed when she complimented me on how well I interpreted it. Like anything else in life, the more you practice a skill, the better you get at it, and the easier it becomes.

Dream

The only thing I remember about the dream is that I was peeling the skin off of my face from a sunburn. The skin was coming off in large portions so I took the skin and weaved it into a beanie type cap that would fit on top of the head. I offered the beanie to a friend who seemed reluctant to accept it after learning what it was made of. I'm curious as to what is the dream interpretation for this very weird dream.

Interpretation

*What an interesting dream that has amazing symbolism! The first symbol I am getting is the peeling of the skin, it is a shedding (like a snake would), which reminds me of a transformation. The sunburn has two meanings. The first is too much exposure to something that is good in moderation, but harmful in excess. The second meaning is being burned by something or someone. The good news is the symbolism of the skin coming off and being woven into a beanie cap. Your dream is showing you that you have **let go** big time of that important lesson because of the large portions of skin coming off of you! The weaving of the cap is really symbolic, for you have learned that lesson well because it is in your head, aka "Thinking Cap." Your offering of the cap to a friend is spreading the knowledge. Unfortunately, not everyone is ready to hear it, as your friend's reluctance showed. Isn't that awesome! I'm sure you know what the lesson is and how it transformed you. I hope this dream interpretation makes sense to you.*

In the following chapters, I will go over the different categories of dreams. You will read many more symbols that are interpreted and clarified according to each dream group. My hope is that the next time you have a dream, instead of grabbing the dream dictionary, you will think about how the symbol relates to what type of dream it was, and how the events that are occurring in your life reveal the true meaning of your dream.

Chapter Two

Environment Dreams

Environment dreams occur during sleeping while we are subconsciously aware of our surrounding environment or our physical body's needs. People chuckle when I mention these types of dreams because they are the easiest to remember. An environment dream usually wakes us up. My personal dreams below will demonstrate this.

Inner Environment Dreams

In my dream I needed to urinate. I went to one stall and there was someone in there, in fact, every bathroom stall I went to was filled, so frustrating. It seemed like forever, however, I finally found an empty one. There was no door! I didn't feel comfortable going because there were men and women hanging around the stall.

My God, Mother Nature was really calling when I woke up! There have been many variations on that dream theme for myself and others. Our bodies will also let us know that we are thirsty in a dream as another dream of mine will show.

In another dream, I was working at a Burger King's soda fountain. In reality, that was my first job at age sixteen. I was so thirsty that I ignored all the soda orders, kept filling my cup, and gulping down soda.

Guess what I did upon awaking?

If we aren't physically feeling well, that can also affect our dreams and you will learn more about that in Chapter Five on Body and Health Dreams. Our reaction to temperature can also have effects on our dreams. When you are cold, your dream could be about snow or ice, being naked, or not being able to find a blanket. The humid weather might cause a dream about being on an island or using a towel to wipe off your perspiration.

Outer Environment Dreams

My clients and most people find these dreams amusing. They do seem rather ridiculous! However, environment dreams are there for our protection. Humans and other living creatures were gifted with the awareness of knowing what is going on in the physical world while we are sleeping. Can you imagine how vulnerable we would be if this did not occur?

These dreams can give us warning that something is not right in our environment. Have you ever watched a cat sleep? Cats are great examples of being warned in their sleep. Humans are alive today because cavemen had this sense. The news is filled with stories of people awakening suddenly when there is a fire or another source of danger. It is too bad that there isn't a study done on what types of dreams they had, although, some may not remember their dreams.

One hot July night, I had left my windows open on the second floor. I had just fallen asleep and quickly awoke to the smell of a horrible body odor. My intuition told me something wasn't right, which triggered fear in me. I got up and looked into the darkness out on the roof. I didn't see anyone, but had the feeling someone was on the roof, so I closed and locked the windows. I figured better safe than sorry and I rather be hot than raped or killed.

Thank goodness, the majority of our environment dreams are funny. When I was in my late teens I worked at a men's clothing store; a co-worker told me about an amusing dream he had while sleeping at the table in our lunchroom. He was dreaming of a large machine that made horrible noises and awoke to see a co-worker (who made the worst noise while chewing) eating his lunch.

A former roommate had the theme of noise integrated into her dream in a different way. She dreamed she was being chased by a very loud piece of machinery. It turned out that a town's workman was using a jackhammer in front of our home.

Here is another outer environment dream of mine:

I dreamed that I was being watched while my chest felt really heavy; it was really creepy and woke me up. Before I opened my eyes, I heard deep breathing. When I opened my eyes there was my cat, Merlin, sitting on my chest and staring at me. I wonder how many pet owners that has happened to?

Sleeping Environment

Your environment plays an important role for sleeping and dreaming. Please do not fall asleep to the television or loud noise. When your environment is quiet, it is easier for your mind to be aware of what is going on in the physical world to keep you safe. A television show or movie can also come into your dreams hours after watching it. Many people fall asleep with the TV on which has a more drastic effect. This is the reason why I won't allow a television in my bedroom because of what happened one time. I was having a nightmare and awoke to hear coming from the television set screams and "Help, he is trying to kill me!"

How is your bedroom or sleeping area? If it is messy, you could have uncomfortable dreams. A client of mine painted his bedroom black, which was a reflection of his life having a lot of issues. He never remembered his dreams; however, intuitively I got that his dreams reflected the turmoil in his life. Would you like to remember your pleasant dreams? A pleasant sleeping environment will help.

You may not want to bother writing your environment dream in your dream journal because it appears to be a no brainer interpretation. I would suggest writing it down because learning your dream symbolism takes a long time. There could be a future dream that uses the same symbol and you will have the proof of the symbol being used in a similar manner.

Chapter Three

Solution Dreams

Dreams have solved many problems in history. Joseph was freed from slavery by the Egyptian Pharaoh to become prime minister, because he interpreted the Pharaoh's dream that saved the country from starvation. Elias Howe patented the first practical sewing machine from a dream which gave him the idea to put a hole near the point of the needle instead of the heel. And Albert Einstein used his dreams all the time to conduct thought experiments to help him revolutionize physics.

Dreams can also give you solutions to your problems. Here is how to use your dreams to get help with an issue. At bedtime, right before you go to sleep, say out loud, pray about, or write down a problem. Ask for a solution to come in a dream and to remember the dream. Keep paper and pen, mobile phone, tablet, or voice recording device close by so upon awakening you can record your dream. When time allows, write it down completely. If not, write down the highlights and the feelings. Feelings are a major clue in interpreting dreams. It may take a couple of nights of asking to get your answer. Or your answer might be meant to be learned during your waking hours. You may occasionally not get an answer because it is not time to know the solution. It is important to trust that it will be revealed when the time is right.

Love Life Questions

I often ask God, my Angels, and Guides for answers in my dreams, which are always useful in my own life, especially for my love life. I encourage my clients to do the same; their dreams are so fascinating to interpret. The following paragraph is from my article "When Will I Find Love" published in SW Experts.

Fifteen years ago I used to live across from the Wharton fire department in New Jersey, US. I often asked a question before going to sleep and got answers in my dreams. One night, I decided to ask my angels and guides, "When will I meet the one?" That night I had a dream where a bunch of fireman were singing the Diana Ross song lyrics about not hurrying love. I awoke laughing hysterically and said – okay, I get it, I'll wait.

I wonder if in real life the fireman could really sing that well in key?

Career and Business Questions

Do you have questions about your career? Is now the time

to go into your own business? Solution dreams to the rescue! I have made major changes in my self-employment because of the answers I got in my dreams. Here is a dream that helped me choose to stop subcontracting for a certain psychic line.

I used to do psychic readings for popular adviser lines. That line was like working at a fast food restaurant. I had one client after another, who wanted their information quickly, and some of them treated me poorly. A psychic friend of mine called those lines "minimum wages for psychics." One night I asked my guides, "Should I leave the line I was currently working for." I dreamed that I was at an old bookkeeping job that I worked for in the early eighties. Yes, I know it's hard to believe I was a bookkeeper, but it is a good skill to know for being self-employed. Even though I learned a lot of lessons from that job, I was very unhappy there. That dream represented my current position and gave me the courage and confidence to leave that line. I have never regretted it.

The next dream from my column *In the Dreamtime* in *Bellesprit Magazine* is a good example of how our personal and business life often are intertwined in our solution dreams. The analysis of this reader's dream can help in both their personal life and career.

Dream
The dream started with me walking through a softball field, like I was invited to be on somebody's team. I didn't really know why I was invited to be on his team. I walked past this one umpire and he looked at me strangely. I walked out into

the outfield in this huge softball complex and everybody was wearing these yellow and white softball outfits. It dawned on me that I was invited to be here because I needed to be on his team. I was all shocked that I was actually supposed to be here, so I started looking for the coach. I went to the umpire and explained the situation to her that I was supposed to be here. She took off her umpire mask, she was what I would call a butch lady with the short hair, and she explained that actually she was the coach. She said let's walk over here. We were walking, she kind of put her arm around my shoulder as we were talking about the team and inviting me on the team.

Interpretation

The main theme of this dream is you have to be a team member. The symbolism of baseball is very American, mainstream, logical, a certain system, and with rules and regulations. Also, each member has their own job, and this works well as a team to accomplish something.

What is interesting is the color of the outfits. The color yellow, interrupted by my guides playing the song, "You Are My Sunshine." What I was going to say is yellow is the color for the solar plexus chakra. The solar plexus chakra is about personal power and needs to be in balance. That my guides gave the sunshine song means that power needs to be bright, sunny, and joyful. I add joy because the Sun card in tarot is all about joy. The color white is about purity and cleanliness. So you must use your power to help people in a pure and joyful manner.

Now, let us put all of the above into the meaning of the

dream. The umpire looking at you strangely is symbolic for being on a team that is not right for you; you may be looked at differently and judged. This could very well be a business environment. The good thing is you walked past him and went into the outfield with a team you are supposed to be involved with. The outfield could be symbolic for something that is "out there." It might not be what you thought it should be; again I am feeling job or a program that helps people. Whatever this group effort is, it will have a feeling of meant to be and you will be welcomed and valued member.

Lastly, the butch woman could mean a few things. The leader of this group will be a butch woman. The leader could be very powerful and creative. Or this group could help balance your male and female side. In other words, bringing your spiritual/creative side into manifestation by taking action.

Unresolved Issues

Solution dreams can help with any area of your life that you have a question about. There are times we get answers in our dreams that we have not asked for because we have either refused to deal with the issue or denied it existed. This could be a current problem or a past occurrence. The Universe doesn't care that you do not want to deal with this subject, yet it is wise and compassionate to the dreamer by using dreams filled with symbolism. These dreams occur a great deal because a large portion of the population is too afraid to deal with current problems or is in denial about childhood issues. It takes a brave person to understand the dream symbolism, and to be courageous enough to deal with and work through the obstacle in order to find freedom from the problem. The following dream sent in to the *In the Dreamtime* column illustrates these types of dreams.

Dream

When the dream started, I was at a gas station with my cousins, but no one had money to get gas, not sure where our money was. But I had 20 dollars in my wallet, so I gave them the 20 bucks to get gas. I knew that wasn't going to get us very far because my uncle said we had 1,400 miles to go. The next thing I know my mom's calling me on the phone telling me to come home because there is a party going on and we can eat food at the party.

At this point my uncle is in the car with me driving us to my house and he turns the wrong way. I try to show him where to turn to go down to my house a different way, but he just speeds past it. We end up in the middle of nowhere when he runs over some guy on the road. My uncle doesn't stop and starts to drive even faster. We come to this old building and he drives the car through the building. There are dead people all along the left hand side of us and then he gets the car stuck, so we have to get out of the car and try to get out of this building.

This woman tells us this is a sacred space. That we're getting sued for going in there and the cops are on the way. So at this point my one cousin turned into my mom, the other two turned into my sister and her friend, and we're trying to get out of this house. This old African American woman then grabs my sister and won't let her go, so I have to go help my sister get loose. Meanwhile, my mom and uncle crawl out the window. My sister and her friend crawl out afterwards. When it's my turn I get half way out the window and I get stuck... I then woke up.

Interpretation

Wow! This is an interesting dream! There is a ton of symbolism and the biggest star are family issues. The first part is where you are going to on the journey of life and your family imprinting is coming with you. You want to go on your own, yet your mother wants you back at home to take care of you. The party symbolizes fun with the family, but also her way to tempt you to the family's way of doing things. The food is nourishment, her taking care of you, because it is at her home and her style of food.

The money appearing when no one had any symbolizes that your needs will be taken care of. Your uncle pointing out how far there is to go represents the family dynamic of making you feel that you won't be able to take care of yourself and look how hard the road is. My guides are responding with, "it's a long, long road" and letting you know your needs are always being taken care of. The long road also shows you have a long life ahead of you.

Your uncle either represents himself, an older male authority figure from childhood, other "bad boys" that have been in your life, or a current boyfriend. Because your uncle is driving the car, it shows how men have taken control of your life. The fact that some men have disregarded what you wanted and told them are shown by him ignoring you. They also didn't follow the rules and don't have much regard for your humanness. In a sense, this man killed a part of you. Most likely your male side (power, logic, and manifestation) was because he did run over a man.

The part of the dream where he gets stuck in an old building means there is a part of you stuck in the past. The dead people on the left hand side could stand for two things. The left side of your body is your intuitive and creative side. Do you have blocks in this area? It could also represent dead issues that have not been completely buried yet.

The woman stating this is a sacred place is referring to the sacredness within you. If you stay in that state you are currently in there will be trouble, hence being sued and the cops coming. Your family members changing into others represent that they all have similar issues, issues you need to work on. Obviously you were a protector of your sister when you were younger.

The fact that some of your family members escaped could symbolize they have gone through their family of origin issues or are escaping from them. It may seem like it was bad that you got stuck in the window but it wasn't. You are halfway (my guides added - a little more) working through your upbringing stuff. My guides said, "To set them free." I also heard a song from the 50's or 60's with lyrics saying "not to worry because everything will be okay." My guides are adding that there is freedom on the other side of it. Many blessings to you.

Answers Using Animal Symbols

People can be in denial of what is going on in their lives and how they are feeling. Or they may know and choose to stay stuck in their current situation. Our dreams will give us a solution in whatever type of dream style or symbolism it can, whether we ask for solutions or not. The following dream from *In the Dreamtime* used an animal symbol to get the point across to the dreamer.

Dream
I had a dream a few days back. I was closing my garage door and there was a white/silver/light colored pigeon in there. It seemed like I needed to let the pigeon out, but it so happened that the garage door closed before I could. The pigeon was still in the garage - and then I woke up. What could this dream mean?

Interpretation
I am intuitively getting that the pigeon is symbolizing love, peace, spirituality, and getting ready to take flight. When I looked up the meaning of pigeon, it also meant family and lessons of the home.

The garage is where you keep a car and I am taking this to mean that you are wanting to travel or move on from your home. Again, I am getting that feeling of wanting to take flight, but in a spiritual way. The garage door closing means that you are feeling trapped, stuck, and not being able to get out.

This dream is telling you it is time to take off! To allow yourself to grow in love, peace, and spirituality. It also could mean that a loved one, be it a family member or friend, also needs to take flight. The dream shows you how the bird (you and/or your loved one) is trapped and needs to be set free. So take the steps to allow takeoffs to happen!

We are here on planet Earth to learn lessons and to grow in loving knowledge. Those lessons are not always fun and easy; in fact, they can be painful. Solution dreams can help you overcome obstacles that are preventing you from growing into your full potential. My hope is this chapter helps you incorporate this style of dreams into your personal growth and life.

Chapter Four

Recurring Dreams

My clients will ask me, "Why do I keep dreaming the same thing over and over again? The dream may not always be the exact same, although it has the same theme - why?" The answer is simple; you have not learned a particular lesson in your life. Humans can easily go into denial about themselves and not want to exert the effort, or are fearful about making a change in order to grow. The subconscious mind does not care about your denial, feelings, nor if you are being a sloth. Therefore, the subliminal mind will remind you in your vulnerable dream state, until that lesson is learned. This is the benefit of recording your dreams: you will begin to notice the repetition, and it will help you understand their meaning.

Recurring dreams for some may seem like a punishment; the reality is it is done out of love to enable your spiritual enhancement. God does the same thing in your waking life; for instance you may attract the same kind of love relationship over and over. This mate can have a different face and name; however, if you never learned how to make boundaries,

your unconscious mind will always attract boundary break-
ers. We not only have recurring dream themes, we also have
recurring life themes along our path of life.

What We Need to Work On

A common recurring dream among my clients is dreaming
about an ex-partner over and over. The dream may have
variations, but their ex is always there. This can represent
a need to move on, forgive, or could represent other issues
within themselves that need to be resolved. It might also
mean that they will see their ex-mate again. In a few cases,
the romance will have a second chance.

One of my clients was so upset about having dreams
about her abusive ex-husband because she was now in a
good relationship with a very loving man. She had done
much inner work on herself and could not understand why
she was still dreaming of him. My guides reassured her the
dreams did not mean she wanted him back, nor would he
come back into her life. The dreams were to help her cut the
final thread of the rope of that type of dysfunctional love to
allow healthy love more fully into her life.

Another reason for recurring dreams is to show us where
we are stuck in life and how we need to take control of our
life. The following dream is a great example of this.

Caller from Radio Show

*A radio show listener called in about the recurring dream
where he often was in the passenger seat of a car. In this*

particular dream he knew the driver, who started driving in reverse causing him to feel trapped and suffocated. He started kicking the door to pry it open so he could escape.

He went on to tell me that in a month he could have up to seven dreams of suffocating or drowning.

Interpretation

His dreams were obviously screaming for his attention. My interpretation of his car dream was that since someone else was driving, he did not feel in control of his life. Cars are great symbolism for our bodies and also how we are traveling in life. The car going in reverse was a great analogy of how he was not going forward in life, perhaps staying stuck in the past. The saying "one step forward and two steps back" really applied to the driving in reverse analogy. To me it was a no brainer that he needed to look at his relationship with this person, because most likely, the person was controlling and/ or it was a very dysfunctional relationship. The silver lining of the dream is he was kicking at the car door, which shows he wants to break out of this pattern.

The drowning and suffocating dreams showed the same thing about not being in control of his life, that he felt like he was dying inside, and barely surviving. My suggestions were to take baby steps to get into the "driver seat" of his life. My guides played the song lyric about looking in the mirror; therefore, it was time to do some deep inter-perspective on his life and where he wanted to go. The drowning and suffocating were also representations of how his personal relationships needed a major makeover.

Phobias in Recurring Dreams

How simpler our lives would be if we could stay the same! We are here on the planet to learn, grow, and evolve. The Earth can tend to be very violent, which comes out in our dreams. For example, being chased by a person or people trying to murder you is a common recurring dream. I also experience these types of dreams. I am usually with a bunch of people and a group of other people are trying to kill us. This has many different scenarios, but often we are hiding. I am sure you can imagine the fear is very intense in these dreams. The good news is they happen less often and I am confronting the people in them. In reality, no one has actually tried to kill me, so this could be symbolic for some of society's rules or something that happened in a past life.

Every human being has some type of phobia that we need to overcome, whether formulated in this lifetime or another. Phobias are not easy to overcome and may appear in our dreams. I knew a woman who was frightened of driving over bridges in her waking life. She had many dreams with the same theme of being on one side of the bridge and she needed to get to the other side. In her dreams she was always terrified of crossing the bridge whether she was driving or walking. There were times she would get a quarter way across, but always turned back. This was symbolic for her career goals; yet, I am also getting intuitively this also included her love life. We have not spoken in many years, I heard through the grapevine that she is doing well. Hopefully, she has reached the other side of the bridge.

The dreams I just described may feel like nightmares to some people; in a sense they are. The nightmare symbolically represents what occurs in our waking life and needs to be addressed. We must face our demons that are holding us back in life for the sake of moving forward in our lives.

Recurring Dreams Mixed With Other Dream Categories

Our recurring dreams may also include other styles of dreams. The next dream comes from a very gifted woman who sent her dream into Bellesprit Magazine. The themes are recurring, precognitive, and lucid dreaming (which is not my specialty), and a great example of someone who is working on their issues.

Dream
In numerous recurring dreams (started about a year ago), I dream I'm dreaming and then dream I wake up. It once happened 3 times. Like I had a nightmare, woke up in my bed relieved it was just a dream, got up and was starting my day, and then woke up again and realized I was still dreaming (got up and met with a friend and told them how they were in the original dream), and then woke up one last time. Each time I woke up it felt so real.

Last night the original dream was that I was doing things with a boyfriend (brown hair, youthful, no one I know). He was a new boyfriend, but we were really close, and I felt comfortable with him. We were with a couple of his friends and looking for a place to stay. We found an apartment that needed some work, but we liked it. My boyfriend and I would be living with these two friends of his, one who is a recognizable TV star (though someone who played a supportive rather than a lead role). After moving our stuff in, it was still daylight, but my boyfriend and I were really sleepy so needed a nap. He took a nap somewhere else in the apartment (we were crashing anywhere since boxes were everywhere).

I fell asleep in the dream and started dreaming I had a child with me (about 4 years old) and was trying to protect it from someone following us. I took the child into a shopping mall to try to lose the person following us (they wanted the child, not me). The dream changed and I was with my boyfriend (from the dream), and it was similar and I felt that same feeling of being followed or being unsafe. He made me feel safe though, and wasn't as worried as I was. Then I woke up (in the dream) and looked at the clock and I had slept 2 hours, it was now dark outside. I was wearing his shirt (white), but it was unbuttoned and I started buttoning it up. I went into the living room and realized his friends were still around and talking to each other. I felt self-conscious since I was only wearing a shirt that wasn't fully buttoned up yet. I was trying to button everything up before anyone noticed and sat down on a couch in the back of the room behind some boxes where I would be less noticeable. My boyfriend woke up and found me in the living room. I was worried he would be mad that I was in there dressed in only his shirt (with other guys around). But he didn't seem concerned. He was really caring, asked me how I slept. We both noted how it was now dark out and we had slept the daylight away. I told him I *had strange dreams and that he was in them. He said hoped it wasn't anything bad (since he was in them). It felt so real, like I was really waking up to talk to him. Then I woke up for real, right before I was able to tell him what the dreams were.*

Appreciate any insight, thanks Pamela.

Interpretation

I heard my guides say the Beatles song title "A Day in the Life" while the instrumental of the song played in the background. Interesting. Please pay close attention to all your recurring dreams and if possible write them down. I am also intuitively getting that you, at times, do some lucid dreaming in your recurring dreams that really makes them feel so real.

My interpretation of the dream is this is symbolic for a man who is coming into your life very soon or has already come in. He feels like a good, safe man. You will be moving forward with him and this could be a permanent lifetime relationship. There is still some cleaning up for you two to do, but both of you are moving forward into a very important role. The moving in together, the boxes that need to be unpacked, needing to rest; all symbolize that this is a process. The supporting star actor is a sign that this is an important relationship and will be very supportive, which was pointed out throughout the dream.

The child you were protecting that you dreamed about within your dream is a representation of your inner child. Your inner little girl feels like it needs to be protected from unsafe people, this feels like people from the past. With this new man your inner child will feel safe.

The fact that you just felt self-conscious, but didn't fear for your safety when you woke up with your shirt unbutton in front of the men, shows that you have done some healing work on yourself. The button-down shirt illustrates that you can be somewhat vulnerable, but can choose how much you want to expose of your life to others. The color white stands for purity and you can be your pure self.

The end of the dream where your boyfriend was caring and supportive about your well-being in the daylight and the nighttime is symbolic that he will be there for you during the light and dark times. He sounds like a good catch.

Near the End of the Lesson

Life is a journey where we process our lessons, and when we get close to the end, there are also signs that we're almost done. The signs may be we feel it is time to move on from a job or person, an issue that always made us upset will no longer make us quite as upset, and of course it appears in our dreams. The following dream that was submitted to my column is a beautiful example of how she is almost at the end. The feeling she felt shows that there is still a little attachment; however, she is at the end of the road and ready to start a new journey.

<u>Dream</u>
I had the same dream twice in one week. The individuals in my dream were people I went to high school with forty years ago and probably haven't seen them but a handful of times in

the forty year span.

I dreamed an individual was deceased and don't recall knowing that individual; however, my high school friend Doris knew him. I could picture her face so clearly and we were in the woods. I recall her being very nice, cute and a cheerleader. She wanted to dispose of his body without anyone knowing. I know it was a male, but don't recall if it was a husband or boyfriend. She wanted myself and another high school buddy to put him in a plastic bag and bury him.

I was popular in school and knew everyone. People started asking me what happened to this individual. One person that asked me was an elderly woman who lived across the street from me in the house when I was married. I've been divorced twenty years and haven't seen her in those twenty years. I remember her being a busybody. One friend that I do stay in touch with, April, (that I used to work with) asked, "Why are you a nervous wreck; what is wrong?" She is one I can always confide in and I told her what I and another friend did. I recall her facial expression in total shock and she said, "This is going to be the death of you...you have ruined your life. What were you thinking?"

It's one of those dreams when you wake up, it's a jerk and your eyes are popping out of your head. Maybe I've been watching the news too much. The exact same dream twice in one week??

Dream Interpretation
If your dream was similar to a television or news show you had been watching and had many of the same characters in

it, than yes it would be an environment dream from watching the news. Yet, the fact that it happened twice in one week and you dreamed of people in high school, a former neighbor, and co-worker – all points to a recurring dream. Recurring dreams are gifts that our subconscious mind give to us to help solve problems and issues in our lives. Let's get on with the interpretation.

Your high school friend, Doris, represents either your past, lessons to learn, or perhaps both. The body of a male represents an old boyfriend or your ex-husband. Another meaning could be the type of man you learned to be attracted to since your high school buddies were helping you. My guides added, "Let go of the old to make room for the new." You were literally putting the old to rest. I would like to add that the fact Doris was a cheerleader meant that you were being cheered on to do this. You are also nice and cute.

The individual that your old school mates and an elderly woman were asking about is in fact **YOU**! How cool is that. They will see the difference in you. May I ask if your former co-worker is negative or stuck in her ways? Perhaps April is judgmental? The question to ask yourself is if you are nervous and afraid of what she and others would think about you? Another thing I would like to point out for you to think about – is it safe for you to confide in her and is she trustworthy?

April is a representation of other people's judgement, as well as your own. My guides are saying, "There is no reason to fear change and being different. Change is good for you." The last thing I would like to point out is when April talks about this being the death of you, that is a symbol of transformation.

Many times people we know become afraid when we transform, which would make us become different. The biggest thing they fear is that your change will make them realize that they are stuck and need to change. Change is scary to many people and they will shame you in order to stay the same.

Lesson Learned

So when does the recurring dream end? When the lesson is learned! There are times when it is very apparent that we got the lessons, yet other times not so much. My dream demonstrates the latter.

In my early to mid-twenties, I had a recurring dream. I was in a small room that had a ton of dressers with all types of drawers. I would open them and find all kinds of treasures. It was so exciting because I never knew what types of riches I would find and they were worth a lot of money. I would stuff the booty into my pockets, my purse, my bra, wherever I could. I was always so disappointed when I awoke.

One day, a few years later, after I had been working with dream symbolism for a while, I thought about my old recurring dreams. I had those dreams before I began my self-growth and spiritual journey. It occurred to me that the treasure hidden away in the drawers was symbolic of the *riches that were inside of me*. What I really had been doing in those dreams was looking for who I was. I then realized that the dreams stopped once I had started on my healing path. Isn't that awesome?

Chapter Five

Body and Health Dreams

Humans are spiritual beings in physical form; we have dreams about our bodies because they are the vehicles that help us experience life. People often take their health and anatomy for granted, sometimes they ignore the signs their body is telling them. The body has a natural preservation and uses dreams to give us information on how to stay healthy, alert us to problems, and provide solutions to our health issues. Here is another good reason to learn dream interpretations if you want insights on how to heal yourself and have good health.

Preventive Care Dreams

A client of mine had a dream that she was surrounded by plates of vegetables, so she started tasting the different types of veggies. I knew right away that she needed to add not only greens to her diet, she also needed to eat a variety of different color vegetables to her diet. This is good advice for everyone, the more colorful the vegetables you eat, the higher amount of nutrition your body receives.

The following is a personal example that happened when I got a sample of herbal tea in the mail. I heard in my head right before I woke up, "Make the tea; it's good for you." I enjoyed the herbal tea as my morning beverage.

Health Care Dreams

Here is how my dreams helped me with female problems that plagued me for years. I'm one of those people that prefer to go the natural way for my health. I have annoyed many medical practitioners. My doctor in New Jersey wanted me to get a hysterectomy, which I was totally against for many personal reasons. One night I had a nightmare about being treated by her and the feeling of being butchered. After that dream, among other things, I was totally against her treating me.

Fast forward a few years, I developed a persistent cough that would come and go. I did all kinds of natural treatments. My sister, bless her heart, was really on my case about going to a doctor. I intuitively felt it was the wrong thing to do. One night I asked my guides if I should seek medical attention for my cough. That night I dreamed that I was in a doctor's office, sitting on an examination table, and a doctor was shoving this metal tube down my throat. I was in absolute terror. I knew there was no way I was going after that dream! Turns out my cough went away when I finally did get a partial hysterectomy, I kept my ovaries. You can call me crazy, but "Ms. Natural" wants to experience menopause.

I was in excruciating pain one day in April of 2012, when my guides told me I would never have a painful period again. I thought they would perform a miracle and I'd get to keep my uterus. I ended up in Carteret General Hospital in Morehead City, North Carolina. I still wanted to hold on to my female parts, until upon waking my guides told me to have the surgery. It was a much more pleasant experience than in Jersey, thanks to Southern hospitality. The dream I had right before I woke up after my surgery confirmed that everything went well and I was Okay. I dreamed that I was typing a letter to the editor raving about my surgeon. Talk about confirmation!

Pregnancy Dreams

This type of dream is very common for women, although I would not be surprised if it happened to men too. My female clients often panic when they have this type of dream, especially if they are not ready or have already raised their children. There is no reason to be afraid, ladies. The following dream was sent in from a woman to my Bellesprit *In the Dreamtime* column.

Dream
I had a dream about being pregnant and I could feel it kick.

Interpretation
Pregnancy usually means about to give birth. It is a time of development, processing, growing, and maturing to be

brought out into the world. Just like fine wine needs to go through the process of grape fermentation before drinking it, so do the majority of things on planet Earth. A difficult concept for us impatient humans to grasp.

In some of my readings I will get a vision or feeling of pregnancy. One time I even felt morning sickness. Yuck! I get a kick out of the women who get really upset because they are not ready to have a baby. Relax, just because you get a message from a psychic or it comes up in your dream doesn't mean you are going to have a baby. Of course, in some cases it does. Another interpretation is a work or house project that needs to be done. Or your spirituality and self-growth could be taking off. Maybe it is a new business? The dreamer knows what is going on in their life.

When you dream that you are about to give birth or actually giving birth this means that the project is almost done. Although, if you really are pregnant with a child, I would keep a close watch or go to the hospital. Once you have given birth to whatever, remember that a newborn needs a lot of care and attention. So make sure you do that with your new project.

My interpretation for the woman who sent me the email is that you have something new coming into your life. It feels like a new phase of life, a rebirth within you that will affect your outer life. The kick you felt was to get going with it.

Dreams about Our Bodies

When someone has dreams about their bodies, it can cause them to become concerned. People can really worry if a nurse, doctor, or hospital appears in the dream. I felt that the *In the Dreamtime* March 2015 column was perfect for this section.

Dream

All I remember about the dream is I with a doctor who was looking at my foot and he said, "You only have 10 months." Then I woke up.

Interpretation

This dream doesn't give me much to go on because it is so short. I also don't know what is going on in your life. However, it is an interesting dream and will give it my best shot.

Feet represent being grounded and that means being present in the moment on the planet Earth. We need our feet to be able to move our body. And our feet also are able to withstand a lot; think about how much weight is on them when we walk.

I wish I knew if it was your right or left foot. The left brain controls the right side of our body which is our logical side and thought of as male energy. The right brain controls our left side of the body which is our creative, intuitive side and thought of as female energy. The reason I mention this is the ten months could be referring to a creative or logical project or pursuit that needs to be done in ten months. Or you may need to pay more attention to your logical side or intuitive side, maybe integrate them better.

I Googled the number ten and there are several meanings – new change, good luck, perfection, pay attention to the guidance from your Angels, to move forward in faith and trust. The number in numerology breaks down into the number one. I get that the number one means being first on the path or beginning a new path. To me, one also means we are at one with everything and what we do has an effect on the whole.

When I look at all of the above, I am getting your dream to mean that a new path is coming for you. It may be difficult to tread at times. But God and the Angels are with you. There may be people who say you can't do this or limit you, that is my interpretation of the doctor's dialog. I am seeing the doctor being used as a mainstream symbolism. That would be in regards to some people with mainstream viewpoints who may see what you are doing with limitations, especially if it is "woo, woo." A doctor's visit can be a turning point but also a healing point in your life. This is a time of transformation for you.

The other interpretation could be taken literally. If you are in ill health, it could mean you are going to die in ten months. However! Doctors are not always right. My Aunt Frieda was in her fifties and the doctors said she would die from breast cancer. She probably outlived some of the doctors and went to the other side at the age of ninety-one!

Are Dreams About Our Bodies Always Literal?

It is very rare that dreams are literal as demonstrated in the above dream. I apologize to my readers who read this column regularly for saying once again – dreams are symbolic and can have several meanings. But it is the truth! There are also different styles of dreams, for example environment, problem solving, or precognitive. A person's life experience and personality add another facet to the interpretation. Dream interpretation is complicated, yet so fascinating!

To go with the theme of our bodies, I will discuss a dream question a client asked me recently without going into all the details. My client had a dream about going blind, and I could tell she was a little nervous about it after giving my take on the dream. So I asked my guides if she was literally going blind.

My guides responded by replying, "You once had a dream about a hole in your head." I forgot all about this dream. I was washing my hair in the shower and discovered a huge hole in the back of my head. It was terrifying! The first thing I did when I woke up was touched the back of my head. That was almost twenty years ago and is my guide's way of saying the dream was not literal. If that dream were literal, I would be dead and not typing this. Honestly, I can't remember what was going on at that time of my life. But what comes to mind are three things. The first is I was not thinking about the whole situation. Secondly, my head wasn't truly together and/or I needed to clean and clear my thinking. The third meaning could be that I was having a dipsy doodle moment.

Are there times that dreams about our bodies could be literal? Yes, of course. For instance, when I had my uterus, I had countless dreams about my moon time coming on. My suggestion to anyone having dreams about their body is to see if the dream recurs and to keep an eye out for any physical changes. You may want to see a medical expert for peace of mind. I wish everyone good health and sweet dreams till the next In the Dreamtime.

Strange Body Dreams

You now understand that body and health dreams are not always literal. Dream symbolism can appear very weird when it comes to our bodies. Our body is also the home for our emotional, mental, and spiritual selves. These next two dreams from my readers for the *In the Dreamtime* column illustrate this point beautifully.

<u>Dream</u>
I dreamed that I was alone in a hospital room feeling sick to my stomach, then I had purplish color eyes. Why do my eyes look that color?

<u>Interpretation</u>
This dream doesn't give me much to go on, but I will give you my best shot. My gut instinct is this dream has something to do with the chakras. Your second and third chakra is off. The second chakra is gut instincts, creativity, feelings, and a connection to your family/tribe. The third chakra is your personal power. I am psychically getting that you are very intuitive and spiritual, but you have blocks to be removed in order to fully be in touch with it. Your purple eye color is your ability to see things in a spiritual way. When you work through your blocks, your third eye will open more.

A humorous way to look at this dream is you feel so sick to your stomach that you see purple.

Dream

This was my bad dream about 2 days ago; I was pulling 2 big cucumber-sized worms out of the top of my head! I threw them on the ground and stepped on them, but they didn't want to die! Then I was back in Hungary in the apartment where I used to live with my parents in the bedroom! My Mother, who has been dead for 17 years, got out of the bed when one of the worms jumped up in the air and she sliced it with a sharp knife! The worm morphed into a black cat and my mother cut off one of its ears! There was blood all over, then I woke up to my own crying!

Interpretation

I was very grateful that I had read your dream after I ate dinner instead of before! Yuck, this dream is a nightmare. But it is meant for your own healing. And really is a gift from your subconscious mind.

The big worms are symbolizing old tapes that are in your mind and/or negative thinking. I would have to say most likely from childhood because the next dream scene was from childhood. The good news is that you have the desire and are getting rid of those negative messages because you are pulling them out. When you are throwing them on the ground, stepping on them, and the worms not dying is symbolic that you want this done quickly. The thing about a quick fix is that it is still there, which is why the worms didn't die. In your waking life you need to go through the healing process to get these issues cleared.

When you dreamed about your old apartment in Hungary

that is symbolic of where your issues started from. The messages of your Mother slicing the worm are how she did her best at helping you and I am interpreting that as also raising you. But she also stifled your independent, individualism, and mysticism – which is shown when the cat's ear is cut off. The good news is that isn't a huge part of you. The ear could mean the way you hear things has been affected.

The blood all over the place has two meanings. The first is how her actions bleed a part of you, which means it stifled and depleted parts of who you are. But the second meaning is she is your blood, your family, and who you are.

I am also getting that your Mother is with you today guiding you, but you are in charge. This dream is encouraging you to look at the past, work through it, and heal from it. My guides just played the Beatles song, "It's Getting Better All the Time." So know that your life is getting better and better. It is time to be who you truly are.

The first dream was a great example of how the eyes really are the seat of the soul and our spirituality. The second dream is more geared to the dreamer's emotional and mental state. Both dreams happened to help their body, mind, emotions, and spirit heal and become healthier.

I hope this chapter inspires you to really pay attention to your dreams and well-being.

Chapter Six

Nightmares

"Anyone out there enjoy having a nightmare?" I'm sure most people would say no because nightmares are scary. When someone is having a nightmare, they could toss and turn, scream out, or end up drenched in sweat. Yet, nightmares are needed to help us get out of denial of a situation or work past a fear to achieve better lives. Bad dreams and nightmares are very similar, except a nightmare will wake you up out of a sound sleep. Nightmares are a gift because the person is being forced awake to look at an issue that they have been avoiding to find a solution. If the person chooses to ignore and downplay the nightmare, it could cause recurring bad dreams/nightmares until the problem is resolved.

Snake Nightmare

A reader sent in their nightmare that used a creature from Mother Nature to my *Bellesprit Magazine* dream column.

Certain species of nature can have an adverse effect during our waking lives that will become nightmares in our dreaming lives.

Dream

I just woke up from a horrible nightmare! I was killing a snake! The snake was looking at me, begging for mercy, and I just kept beating him on the head. I then put him in a plastic bag and threw him in a muddy water pond.

Interpretation

There are four meanings for snakes, the first is shedding of the old in order to transform. Health is the second meaning because snakes are used as a symbol for the medical profession and the rising of the kundalini which normally stays dormant and coils at the base of spine. The third one is from the story of Adam and Eve for temptation. A man's penis is the fourth symbolism of a snake.

I will give three possible meanings for the dream:

- *One meaning could be that you are resisting letting go of the old or a health issue. You are beating yourself up over it and feeling unclean because of it. If this is the case, please allow yourself to transform and heal.*
- *Another interpretation is for a temptation in your life. This temptation keeps appearing in your life that is symbolized by the snake looking at you. There are all kinds of rationalizations for this temptation, which is when the snake begs for mercy. You know that you need to beat this and get rid of it.*

- *The last interpretation is the symbolism for a man and/or sexuality. You can determine if this is the meaning by asking yourself the following questions. Is there a man who is trying to be in your life that you are resisting? Are you angry at a man? Do you want all men out of your life? The last question to ask yourself is do you think sex is dirty?*

This nightmare is a great example of how a symbol can have many different interpretations in a dream. I often give two or more different meanings to my readers and clients; the reason for this is that the dreamer will intuitively know which interpretation fits best in their life.

Evil Characters in a Nightmare

The following nightmare is a personal dream from a couple of decades ago. This dream has always stayed with me because it helped me find a solution in helping me with my nightmares. In the past, when I had a nightmare I would fall back asleep and go right back into the horror. Or I would stay up terrified to go back to sleep. This dream also appeared in one of *In the Dreamtime* columns.

Nightmare
Nightmares are the worst! Whenever I have one, there is no way I can fall back asleep without going back into the same dream. But nightmares are there for a reason, they help us overcome an issue. When my niece was three I had the

following dream:

My niece, Cynthia, and I were in a basement of a home that I used to live in with roommates. We were talking when I heard an evil cackle of a witch in the back of the cellar. I was terrified and wanted to escape from there. I said to Cynthia, "Let's get out of here." I reach to grab her, but instead she walks away from me toward the laughter. I was frozen on what to do. Part of me wanted to run away to safety. But I couldn't just leave my niece there.

I awoke from the dream. I was shaking with fear and knew if I fell asleep I would go right back into that nightmare.

Facing the Nightmare

I went into a state of meditation and recalled the dream. I visualized myself running and catching up to Cynthia before she got to the witch, stopped her, and grabbed her hand. The witch looked like the evil witch from "The Wizard of Oz." Hey, I feel your smiles and giggles, but it's my visualization and I used whatever worked. I told her to leave us alone. The witch did her cackling laugh and went towards us. I turned around, grabbed a bucket of water, and threw it on her. The drenched witch started yelling, "I'm melting, I'm melting." We watched her melt away. Cynthia looked up and smiled at me. We turned around and walked hand in hand out of the basement.

I came out of my visualization, laid back down, and slept like a baby.

Interpretation

My niece is now in her mid-twenties, but I remember this dream like it was yesterday. When Cynthia was a young child she represented my inner-child. The basement is a low-level place, has always been creepy for me, and where the root of the problem was. The evil witch was symbolic for my fearful, dark side. I was in turmoil of whether to face my demons and free my inner-child issues. Or take the easier, wimpy way out and run.

When I went into meditation I had no idea how I was going to proceed. The love I felt for my Cynthia and my inner-child (I had an established relationship through prior work) gave me the courage to face the witch aka "My dark side." I spoke my truth, even when I knew she meant us harm. By throwing the water on her: I was cleansing away my fears, the dirtiness I felt about myself, and not letting my past issues have any power over me. When Cynthia and I walked out of the basement, we were walking into a new phase of our lives.

The mediation I did was a very quick and powerful solution to the nightmare; and best of all I was able to go back to sleep. There was still work that I needed to do in my personal healing, however; the meditation gave me the courage to work on the self-growth. I hope that my experience will encourage you to look at any future nightmares and to try a guided meditation to find a solution.

People Attempting to Harm You Nightmares

The following nightmares come from May 2014 *In the*

Dreamtime column. The first dream is from a submission by a reader. The next dream is a personal dream. I also give solutions that can help you when a nightmare occurs which I felt were a perfect way to close this chapter.

Nightmare

You know, it's funny, I very seldom dream, but last night I dreamed someone was trying to kill me. Scared me so badly that it woke me up and I never went back to sleep. Crazy!

Interpretation

This dream may seem crazy, but it is quite common. It is also understandable why you wouldn't want to go back to sleep. Because intuitively it felt safer in case you went back into the nightmare or were afraid someone was really after you. It is hard for me to give you the exact interpretation for three reasons. One - it was little information to go on. Two - I don't know your history. And three – I constantly remind my readers and clients that you are the best interpreter of your dreams, I am just a guide. The following are different meanings of the dream:

- *You are in danger, **but intuitively I am getting that is not the case**.*
- *Someone is hurting you and you need to protect yourself mentally, emotionally, physically or spiritually.*
- *An ending of something in your life is, will be, or was uncomfortable to go through.*
- *You are remembering a past life.*

My Dreams and Solutions

In my late twenties, I used to get dreams of men trying to hurt me. Some of the dreams were telepathic communication of what he was going to do me, and I would be terrified. Other dreams would be me running away from someone.

It got to the point where I was scared to sleep alone in my home. I was grateful that I had two roommates because someone was always home, except for one night when both of my roommates were away. I was terrified to go to sleep because of what I might dream or that someone could break in and hurt or kill me. Finally, I was so exhausted at three am in the morning that I got down on my knees and prayed. I still remember my prayer – "God, if it is thy will that someone comes in and rapes or kills me, thy will be done. But I'm tired and going to sleep now."

I can laugh about it today, but at the time it was really scary. That prayer helped, yet what really helped was working on my childhood issues and going through the healing process. Since that time I have lived alone in three different homes and loved it.

Occasionally, I will get dreams with the recurring theme that people are trying to kill me and my friends/family. We are running and hiding. I cannot prove that theme refers to a past life. However, my gut tells me it is, and as a psychic that is good enough for me. The good news is the more empow-ered I have become in myself, the more it changes the dream. When I do dream of being hunted, I fight back and feel more confident in myself.

Here are some solutions that will help you with these types of dreams aka "Nightmares":

- *Upon waking, ask God, the Angels, Jesus, the Great I Am, (whomever you feel comfortable with) to protect you.*
- *It helps me when I visualize tigers, lions, black panthers, and leopards surrounding my home to protect me, too. You can use whatever makes you feel better. Hey, I just got a great idea! In the future I will use Jason Statham with a machine gun guarding my home. Nothing like a little eye candy to help with a nightmare!*
- *If you cannot get back to sleep, meditate that you are back in the dream in a state of power to conquer whatever demons you need to.*
- *Look deep within to see what could be causing this.*
- *Start journaling your dreams and write down any past dreams. You will discover a theme.*
- *It is important for you to continue on the path of self-growth and deal with your issues. We all have stuff that we need to clean up or we would not be here on Earth.*

Finally, you may need a professional to help you. It could be someone like me – psychic, coach, and dream interpreter. You may prefer a trusted clergy member, coach, therapist, or a group environment. Whatever method you choose, my hope is that your nightmares turned into sweet dreams!

Chapter Seven

Deceased Loved Ones in Dreams

Every living creature must depart into the unknown at the end of their lives, and their departure leaves their living loved ones filled with grief. This is a natural stage of existence. For those who have no belief in an afterlife, the loss of their loved one can be very devastating. Others who have a belief in an afterlife grieve while hoping the departed are in a better place. Mediums, others, and I who have been visited by those who crossed over – *know there is an afterlife.* We still need to go through the normal grief process, although it is easier for us because we can have occasional visits. Our deceased loved ones visit us in many different ways.

Our departed ones visit us through our feelings. Have you ever sensed a dead one's presence? They may touch us, we may see them out of the corner of our eyes, or smell them. How can we smell them you might wonder? You could smell a cologne they once wore, if they baked cookies you would smell cookies, or if they were an alcoholic you may smell booze. Obviously, if you walk by a bakery most likely it is not your Aunt Emma saying hello. My Mother was a very heavy smoker, I am one of those ex-smokers who detests smoking. You are not allowed to smoke in my presence, let alone in my car or home. When my Mother first passed, I often smelled the scent of cigarette smoke in my car while driving alone. I knew it was her and would say hello. It still happens occasionally. She often requests that I leave an oldie song that comes on the radio, when I would normally click to another station.

Another way those who crossed over communicate to us is you may hear their voice in your head, or hear a song they liked over and over. I heard the song "Judy in Disguise" all the time on a variety of radio stations and at different times of the day after my Mother died. Her name was Judy. Another way those who have died communicate is by moving things, playing with the electricity, or a change in the room temperature.

The easiest way for them to communicate with us is through our dreams. There are thousands of stories of how a deceased loved one visited someone in their dreams. This happens to reassure us that they are all right. Why do they visit us in their dreams? It is the easiest way for them to visit us. Here is an analogy to help you understand this: imagine that you are deep in the forest, and you are on your mobile phone trying to connect to the internet without Wi-Fi. How hard would that be? Now, you exit the forest and there is a free Wi-Fi coffee shop, you are now connected to the internet. The coffee shop represents our dream state.

To help you understand this further, the following is a

question a reader asked *In the Dreamtime* column in Belles-prit Magazine.

Question

I have very vivid dreams with deceased loved ones. They are very real. Is it a dream or a visitation? How can you tell?

Answer

This is a question that I get asked a lot. My feeling is the majority of your dreams are visitations. The fact that you mention that they are very real to you is a sign that you really feel them. Granted, we feel in all dreams, but not all dreams feel so real.

There are a couple of ways to tell if it is real. Feelings are important to differentiate if it is real or not. A great example of that is if the emotion of love is very beautiful and intense in a way that has never been felt before in your waking or dream state. I personally have experienced it; words cannot describe this wondrous love.

The feeling of peace and reassurance is another sign that the dream was real. Many of my clients have said that the night or a few days after a loved one had passed they were visited by them - often to let them know they were OK and ready to move on. My cat, Midnite, did this.

It does not have to be a recent departure that one who has crossed to the other side comes for a visit to give you peace and reassurance. If you are having trouble letting them go or have another issue in your life, your deceased loved one will come to help you.

Another way to know that it was a visitation is that they came by to say hello, had a brief conversation, or to simply hang out with you. There is NOT much action. Many times upon awakening you will forget the conversation. A personal example is when I was twenty, I dreamed of my friend, Winnie, who had been killed in a car accident three years before. She was on my back porch and said my nickname and hello. That was it, but I knew in my heart that it was real upon waking.

Sometimes, your loved ones may use a symbolic dream to get a message to you. Most of these dreams are very short. They may have trouble using words and it is easier for them to use a symbol.

An important fact to know is that those who have crossed over have a much higher frequency than those who reside in the physical plane. We need to be at a much lower vibration in order to remain in a solid form. When we are in the sleep/ dream state our vibrations raise up and it is easier for those in the higher realm to interact with us.

The way to tell that it is not a visitation is that the dream flashes from one scene to another scene, or many scenes. The dream has a ton of symbolism, makes very little sense, and/ or is totally wacky. You could also dream of a past event that brings up a lot of unresolved feelings with your departed one. That is a sign that there are issues you need to work on and let go. Another way to know is that the dream feels like an ordinary dream. There is a different feeling when you have a visitation that is hard to describe. It is a knowing that it was more than a dream. I hope that helps.

Death of someone we love is hard for many of us. The ones who have passed have returned **home** and are joyful to be back in its love and light. Those in spirit form are happy, it is the ones left behind that are sad. They come to visit us in our dreams to let us know they are well or to finish anything that needs to be resolved. When a child dies, death by an accident, or someone is murdered – the grief is intensified. We want to know why and have many questions. The next dream from one of my column reader demonstrates this.

Murder Dream

My brother was murdered, I had a dream my brother was trying to tell me what happened, and he was just saying the same thing over and over. He was saying it was not supposed to go down like that and he was saying his head was hurting. He also said that he knew the people who did this to him. Then he was acting like he was still alive and laughing.

Dream Interpretation

Before I go into the interpretation, I would like to say I am sorry for your loss. It hurts when we lose a loved one through natural causes and accidents, I'm sure the grief is magnified when someone we love is murdered. My guides are playing Michael Jackson's song, "You Are Not Alone," that means that you are surrounded by your Angels, guides, ancestors, and God.

This dream sounds like a visitation dream to me. It is easier for loved ones who crossed over to visit in our dreams because our energy is higher; therefore, it is not as difficult for those on the other side to visit with us. Your brother is letting you know in this dream that the murder was not premeditated, could have been prevented, and he knew the people who killed him.

The head hurting could mean three things. The first is he died from a head injury. He had a headache or was confused at the time of his death could be the second meaning. The third meaning may be referring to your state of mind concerning his death.

Your brother's most important message was letting you know that he is still with you and is happy. His laughter is his way of saying, "Hey, I'm Okay and I want you to be happy." I will keep you and your brother in my prayers.

When I interpreted this dream I could feel her brother with me. He wanted his sister to know he was happy, not to dwell on his murder, and to move on with her life. I know it is easy for him to say because he is not stuck in the Earth plane like we are. The main point was to start the healing process.

Symbolism vs Visitation

Not every dream we have of a deceased person is an actual visitation. Our dreams help us to resolve unresolved issues and often we have unfinished business with the departed. A person may dream screaming at their parent because they were cruel to them as a child. Or a parent whose child died may have recurring dreams of trying to save their child from a life threatening situation. These upsetting dreams are your way of healing these issues.

I mentioned earlier in a dream interpretation the way to know dreams are actual visits is that they feel like a visitation. The conversations are short, there may be no words, not much action is occurring, and there is feelings of love and peace. The next dream that was sent to my *In the Dreamtime* column is a great example of how a dream is not an actual visitation from her deceased Mother. Or is it?

Dream

I am the youngest of 6 siblings. My mom passed away when I was in my early twenties in 1986, she was 59. I am a person that very seldom remembers my dreams. My dream last night has puzzled me as I have sat and thought about it over and over again shaking my head. It was so clear, but yet I don't understand what I am being told.

Here it goes:

I was entering a building that was a nursing home to visit my brother who was there recovering from some surgery, but I don't know what type it was. As I entered the building there were a set of full glass, double doors. There was a wide concrete sidewalk leading up to the door. Many trees shading the area. Once in the building it was darker, till I walked around to the right and down this one hallway to David's room. This area was white and bright like a hospital, etc. As I am heading down the hallway, I saw his name on the wall near his door. As I was going to turn to my right to enter his room, I saw to my left a door with my mother's name on it. I stopped, felt shocked, and walked to the doorway. I could see her lying in her bed. But I couldn't enter.

Then the dream jumped to me trying to find the manager of the home because I was told I couldn't see her. She didn't want to see me. So of course I am now crying. (I am an adult in this dream and my mother was older than what I remember her before she passed.) In the dream I am walking around the building everywhere trying to get help. I then went to this waiting area and sat down, then my mother came into the room. I stood up, then we sat back down. Her left hand up to her elbow was bandaged up in a tan colored wrap. She was slimmer than when she was alive and a little taller. I was also an older adult. (It's like it was current time and age.) She sat down to my left; we were on a unit like a love seat with a cushion. We talked about things. I kept asking her why she didn't want to see me. How long she had been there. I told her how much I loved her and missed her. I said I have so many questions. She held my hand and then I woke up before I could get the answers.

Thanks for all your help. I normally can't remember dreams once I wake up, but this one is still there. Very clear.

Interpretation

Thank you for sending in this dream. Your dream is loaded with symbolism regarding your mother's passing. The path to enter the hospital is leading you to a journey of healing with two of your family members. The shading of the trees and the darkness of the hospital and walking into the brightness is an analogy of bringing issues out of the darkness into the light.

Your brother, David, has issues that need to be worked on. Since he is recovering from surgery in your dream, he must be working on them. Or it is your opinion and feelings that he needs help and healing. Your mother's room being right next to your brother is symbolic of them being close to one another. I am also feeling intuitively that you had problems with their relationship.

There is another interpretation to your brother and mother's room being side by side that I feel uncomfortable saying. It could also mean that your brother is next in line to cross over to the other side. It is up to you to decide which one makes the most sense.

The part where she is in the bed, but you could not enter means that she has always been around you even though you didn't see her. The not being able to enter means not being able to visit her in heaven. The part where she doesn't want to see you represents your inner child that felt she left you, not logical, but our inner child is more illogical. The running around for help is your willingness to get help in this department. But you also surrender and sat down in the waiting room.

When your Mother does come to you, I am feeling psychically that was a real visitation. The fact that she looked different is also a sign of how she has changed on the other side. She also came to help you resolve your subconscious unresolved feelings towards her passing. I have no idea of what the bandage means, perhaps it is a personal family message? The love seat symbolizes your love and closeness. The fact that she sat on your left side shows that you were using more of your intuitive self. The conversation feels real. And of course, there are always unanswered questions.

The fact that you normally do not remember dreams shows that this was a very important one! First, for you to be aware of that there are unresolved issues around your brother and mother's passing to be healed. Second, the visit was real because you remembered it so well.

This dream shows how we humans always have issues to work on. But, what is really awesome about this dream is that it shows us that we are always and forever connected with our loved ones!

Warning Dreams of Upcoming Deaths

I need to make an important point before I go into warning dreams. There are people who believe that animals do not have a soul, which is a load of garbage! All living things have a soul, have lessons to learn, and evolve. If they breathe, eat, discard waste, feel, love, and have a form of communication (even if we can't understand it), why would they not have a soul like humans?

People often have dreams alerting them that someone close to them will have an upcoming death. These dreams can be a gift and a curse at the same time. The gift is being able to make amends and/or say goodbye. It feels like a curse because the majority of the times you cannot stop it. This type of dream has happened twice in my life.

My cat, Midnite, and I had a very special relationship where we communicated easily with one another. Midnite was the only one that could ever go inside my head and psychically hit against my skull from the inside. It was the strangest sensation and she would do it when angered at me for not paying enough attention to her. This cat was super spoiled!

One night I had a dream that Midnite was in the enclosed porch where my roommate's dog usually was. I wanted to keep her safe and away from harm; therefore, I started to nail wooden boards to keep her from coming out. I had a feeling of relief that she could not get out and was safe, when she popped out of the sealed door. Midnite went off to be with a variety of other animals; I was left with a feeling of abandonment and sadness.

I awoke very sad because I noticed that Midnite's behavior had changed; lately she spent more time in my roommate's room, and was not waking me up in the morning. I took a shower crying hysterically because I did not want my cat to pass. She knew how upset I was and came into the bathroom to comfort me. My denial and hope kicked in that maybe she would not die, but every time I did a tarot spread, it showed endings. Midnite ended up dying in my arms as I held her heart against mine.

I could not bury her that day because the ground was frozen, I did not have a shovel, and had to wait for my roommate to do it the next day because he worked that night. Midnite's body was in a box in my room when I finally fell asleep. That night I dreamed (or did I?) the following:

I awoke to her meow and rubbing up against my legs, I put my arms out to grab her in order to hold her. She jumped up to the windowsill, went through the window, and disappeared into the sky.

Midnite often visited me during waking and dreaming time. Nine months later, I adopted my all white cat, Merlin. *One night I dreamed that Midnite stepped down from a pedestal and Merlin climbed on top!* I'm sure you can understand that meaning. A year or so later I adopted Rhiannon, who looks like Midnite and has many of her characteristics.

Does knowing someone we love is going to die make the grief process easier? The answer varies with each person. If you dream of someone dying does that mean they are going to die? Not always, sometimes it can mean that they are and/or your relationship with them is transiting into another phrase in life.

When someone dreams of visitations to the other side is that scientific proof that it was an actual visit and life goes on? Of course not; that is for every human being to determine. My hope is that it brings you comfort, helps you to see how precious life is, and for you to enjoy being alive knowing that you will see your loved ones again.

Chapter Eight

Precognitive Dreams

Precognitive dreams are premonitions of upcoming events about to happen in your waking life on Earth. This style of dreams is my favorite because they prepare and help me for upcoming events. Precognitive dreams tend to be more vivid, are usually easier to remember than other dreams, and convey an inner knowing that this will occur in the future. A few precognitive dreams show the future close to the way it happens. The majority of these dreams are shown in symbolism and need to be analyzed. Other precognitive dreams need future events to happen before you can register the type of dream it was and comprehend the meaning. In this chapter I have four precognitive dreams to analyze. The first three are my personal dreams and the last dream is from *Bellesprit Magazine*.

Close to Actual Events Precognitive Dream

I had the following dream in my late twenties.

I was in my grammar school gymnasium surrounded by lots of people. There was a nice looking man with dark hair, a beard, and mustache. I do not remember the words, but the feeling I got was that he wanted to control me. I felt like I needed to get away from him.

A few months go by, then I was at a party and the man who was in my dream introduced himself to me. I was shocked, talked to him, and foolishly gave him my phone number. He pursued me very hard and would stop by the places he knew I frequent. I went out on one date and got the same feeling I did in the dream. That date was an important lesson for me because I realized that the dream I had was indeed a premonition to warn me to not become involved with this man. I kept my distance and thankfully he got the hint. I found out later that although he was in his late twenties, he had been married three times! He obviously had issues with relationships and I had no intention of being wife number four.

The dream was short but it illustrates how important feelings are in dreams because in my waking life the man brought up those same feelings. You need to know that it is rare to dream of a stranger and for them to look actually like that in real life. The gymnasium represented three things. The first was all the people in the gym were for the upcoming party that I was going to attend. The second was it was in my old grammar school and I was still young at learning healthy relationship skills. The third symbolism is that relationship would have been one crazy undertaking.

Symbolic Precognitive Dreams

My next two dreams were symbolic for upcoming events. The first of the two dreams is a wonderful example of how we have free will to make changes in our life. In 1992 I was working as a bookkeeper at a car dealership. I really disliked my job, and here is my dream about my place of employment.

I had just finished watching the first part of a movie and was very excited to watch the second half. A couple of the salesmen and the service manager were there. One of the salesmen told me not to bother watching the second half - that it was not worth it. I was upset and angry because I really wanted to watch it. I looked over to where the service manager was sitting, then the bottom of service manager's shoe really stood out, I noticed there was a hole and another little hole was starting.

I woke from that dream knowing exactly what it meant because I had been working with symbolism of dreams for a number of years. The first part of the movie was my life up to then. The second part of the movie was what my life could be like in the future. The salesman (who represented certain people and also mainstream ideas) telling me not to bother meant to stay stuck where I was, which made me upset and angry because I was unhappy there. The holes in the service manager's shoe were the analogy that the job was giving me a "hole in my soul," and the little hole symbolized that if I stayed the damage to my soul would only get worse. After I had that dream I continued my education in the healing and psychic arts. In 1993, I left that job and began my own private practice.

The next dream I had around 2010 really confused me. I thought I had interpreted it correctly, but it was only after certain events happened that I got its meaning.

I dreamed that I was upstairs in an office building looking at an office to rent. It looked like a combination of offices that I had rented in Morris County, New Jersey. The office needed to be cleaned up and part of the floor was unsafe and required repair. I continued walking into another room and noticed there was some old furniture that needed to be thrown out. I walked back into the other room and there was my sister happily hammering away at some new boards in the floor.

A few weeks later I looked into renting office space in Boonton, New Jersey (that was on the second floor) for workshops. I felt that was what the dream meant. Fast forward a few months. After a series of unfortunate events, it became evident that it was time for this Jersey girl to leave New Jersey because I could no longer afford the cost of living there. I decided to move in temporarily with my sister in North Carolina. I gave away my old furniture because I was moving to the furniture capital of the country. It was cheaper to buy new stuff than the cost of moving it and storage. I lived there for a month when it occurred to me what the dream meant.

The combination of the offices in NJ meant I was taking my knowledge with me and moving my business. The need to clean up and get rid of furniture was what I had to do when I left my old place. And my sister hammering away at the floor was symbolic of her helping me with the foundation of living in North Carolina. How awesome was that! I stayed at my sister's home for six months before going on my own. I miss certain things in New Jersey but not the traffic or shoveling snow. I am content being a "Damn Yankee" in North Carolina.

Precognitive Dreams for World Events

Friends and clients often tell me they had dreams foretelling earthquakes, tsunamis, 9/11, or heinous crimes and had no idea what it meant until after the actual event. They sometimes feel guilty because maybe they could have stopped it. If people were meant to stop the actual event, they would have. Just like dreams of a loved one's upcoming death, these dreams are trying to give us a heads up of an upcoming event to help alleviate the trauma.

The following is a great example of a precognitive dream that appeared in July 2013 *In the Dreamtime*.

<u>Dream</u>

This is the weirdest dream I ever had. I was in a village, a woman came up to me and said that St. Bernadette would like to talk to me. The village was like in a third world country. So I went to the altar that was made for her. I felt her talk to me through my chest. She said that she wanted to destroy a village. So I pleaded with her that the way of Christianity is to forgive. I said that if she destroyed the village men, women, and children would be destroyed. So I immediately went to a house in the village and started to clean up hoping that the village would be spared. I saw a large metal box (almost like a freezer) in the middle of the living room. This box had stagnant water so I thought I would throw away the water, clean up the box, and have it removed. As I went towards it, St. Bernadette flew up from behind the altar and said not to interfere with her remains, because that is her remains. She had on her blue gown. She said she did not like anyone interfering with her remains. It was as though she had a direct connection to where her remains were. Then I think I saw where her body was lying. Then I awoke. But I did not want to be awaken so I closed my eyes trying to go back. I saw her hovering in my bedroom in another dream that was short.

So that morning I had an appointment to see a Catholic Priest concerning my marriage (we were forbidden to have the Eucharist as my wife is a divorcee but just received the approval). He told me that was not St. Bernadette, as she does not have that kind of authority. Later I started to pray for this village and said that if they could not be spared that they be taken painlessly. That weekend, two villages in the Philippines were swept away in a flood at 2am in the morning. CNN said that the people were all asleep so they did not have the chance to escape. I did research concerning the Philippines and realized that it was not "punishment" but like a rapture. They were taken because of the problems of exploitation. Also I recently found out that the Pope freed a priest accused of interfering with children. Apparently they do not care about the people. Of course, the Pope resigned.

I have had dreams of things that have happened in

America, e.g. the attack on the children at the school, but it was not guns but a bomb in a soda machine. However, I saw in a dream a letter that America does not like to take things like these from "outsiders" as such. Since then I have received no more dreams. I invite your opinion on what I experienced.

Interpretation

Thank you for that awesome example of how a precognitive dream has lots of symbolism. The reason for that is because the language of the dreamtime is not the same as when we are awake. And some things may be too disturbing for the dreamer to actually see happening.

St. Bernadette was a representation of Mother Earth, or if you prefer the term, Goddess. She was talking to you through your heart chakra. She was showing you a vision of an upcoming event that was humanly impossible to change, although you tried. The stagnant water is showing that the energy in the village must be cleansed. She made it clear that she must do it this way and humans may not interfere. The remains symbolized her Earth body. Her gown was the color blue, which is many people's favorite color. Blue is the color of the sky (heaven and the intellect) and water (cleansing and emotions) which is perfect for the dream.

I am picking up that you will have more of these dreams in the future. It may, at times, feel like a burden and curse because you cannot make a dramatic change in the upcoming events. That is not completely true. Your prayers helped those two villages. I am hearing and feeling Mother Mary. Not only does she want you to pray for upcoming events, but she wants you to get other people to pray, too. Some people will think you are crazy, but not the people at Bellesprit and other groups. Mother Mary is saying, "We are here to help." So pray to be shown to the people whose prayers can also help soften these upcoming tragedies. It is a gift even if it doesn't feel like that. Many blessings to you.

Precognitive dreams are another great reason to keep a record of your dreams. You might not recognize at the time that your dream is predicting the future. When the actual event occurs, there will be proof because you have written, typed, or made a voice recording of your dreams with the date. Another asset of documenting your dreams is it will be easier to recognize future precognitive dreams. I hope you use the information wisely!

Chapter Nine

Spiritual Dreams

Human beings are on the Earth plane in order to grow into higher spiritual beings. We do this from the lessons that occur on Earth. Our lesson plans consist of how we treat other humans and all living creatures, pursue goals, overcome obstacles, and work on personal growth. No one said the journey is easy and dreams show where we are currently at on our path's destination. Spiritual dreams are meant to comfort us during difficult times, show us how much we have grown, and encourage us to go to a higher level.

Some of you may think that everything occurs in our waking and dream life is spiritual, and I cannot argue with you because in a sense it is. What makes spiritual dreams stand out is that there could be spiritual characters, like Jesus or Buddha. In spiritual dreams you will be afraid to do something, yet will go through the experience. The last element of these dreams is that you will be leaving one chapter to advance to the next level in your life.

Spiritual Healing Dreams

My clients often tell me they dream of an angel, Jesus, or spiritual beings healing them. Here is one of my dreams that happened in the nineties during an emotional time in my life.

I was laying on a table surrounded by three spiritual beings, one at my head, and the other two were on each side of me. Everything seemed to be in the color purple. There was a feeling of safety and love emanating from them that made me feel safe and calm. They told me they were doing surgery on my heart to help heal it.

When I woke up it seemed like it was an actual visit and my heart area ached for a couple of days; however, it felt much clearer. The healing helped me open up my heart a lot more.

Shot in the Head Dream

The following dream from January 2013 *In the Dreamtime* is a personal dream I had a few days before writing my first dream column in *Bellesprit Magazine*. There is no coincidence that this dream occurred right before New Year's or my first column; it was meant to be.

I was at a party when a man with bad energy came in and pointed a gun at me. I was scared because I wanted to live and not die. He shot me in the head. I couldn't believe I was dead because I still felt alive. I went up to people I knew, but they didn't see me even though I talked to them lovingly while gently touching them.

I went over to the two cats on the coffee table, one was orange. I petted the other one and to my joy I was able to understand what the orange cat was saying. Two men went by me and to my surprise they could see me. "You can see me?" One of them responded, "We are dead too." I instantly got that they were a part of the gang run by the man who shot me and he had killed them also. I got a wave of a bad energy. They tried to stop me, but I pushed my way by them and left the house.

I was walking down the street when I saw a Golden Retriever coming towards me. I bent down to pet him, which he was happy to accept. I was disappointed that I couldn't communicate with him like I did with the cats.

I went around a corner and saw three huge beautiful Goddesses. The energy was incredible, so loving and beautiful. I was in awe, knew this was where I belonged, and was a part of. As I got closer, more women approached from a different direction. And a woman was dancing gracefully in a long, flowing gown. I stood in front of the Goddesses. I had so many questions, but knew I needed to wait for my questions to be answered.

Interpretation

There are people who think that if a person dies in a dream, for example falls off a cliff and hits the bottom, that person will die in real life from the shock. I can't help but wonder how they would truly know that if the person did die that way, unless a medium told them. This is the second dream that I have been shot in the head and obviously the shock did not kill me. Believe me, it is very frightening getting shot in the head in a dream. My first experience was in 1992. In the 1992 dream, the planet was overpopulated and would kill you if your social security number was called. They called my number, I told the man with the gun that I didn't want to die. He responded, "You have no choice, turn around so I can shoot you." I told him no, to shoot me while I was looking at him. He shot me in the head and I didn't die. That dream was a symbolic precognitive dream because about six months later I went through a major transformation, leaving the so-called comfort of a mainstream job to start my non-mainstream business.

In my recent dream where I got shot in the head and died is symbolic of the death of an old way and the birth of the new. At this time, I was changing my direction in my personal practice and undergoing a personal transformation because of it. The people who could not see me, although I care about them, represent that some people will not get nor be ready for this work. The two bad energy men are symbolic for a couple of clients that I had to make boundaries with and let go of in order to move down my path.

The cat and the dog could mean a couple of things. I love dogs, but cats are my heart, my soul mates. It is much easier for me to relate and understand cats over dogs. Cats also represent mystery, intuition, and independence. Orange is the color of the second chakra, which is intuition, creativity, and sexuality. Dogs represent unconditional love. It is most interesting in this dream because love is more of a feeling than verbal communication.

The three Goddesses could represent the maiden, mother, and crone. At the age of fifty I am getting closer to being a crone. Yay, wise woman! Because I came from a different direction than the other ladies, it could mean working with groups of women. Another interpretation is I am going into a higher level of female spirituality and have so much to learn. Or it could mean all three, which feels right to me.

Car in the Water Dream

The reader who sent this dream to *Bellesprit Magazine* is a recovering alcoholic, and is a great representation of where they were in their recovery and life. This dream also shows the person walking through their fear, speaking up, and ready to embrace their future.

Dream

I dreamed that I was driving my car and turned my head to look at the upcoming left turn. I used to take that turn to go to AA meetings. Because I wasn't paying attention, my car veered off to a lake that was on the right. This lake is not there in real life. I tried to avoid going in the water, but did, and was so upset because the car was only a couple of years old. I knew I should leave the car so I wouldn't go under, but couldn't bring myself to leave it. The car floated to the edge of the river and ended up going down a chimney into a fireplace.

I'm inside someone's house, but didn't feel afraid they would yell at me for trespassing. I shouted out, "Hello" to let them know I was there. I found a door and was in their backyard. It was filled with all these biker guys, at first I felt afraid because I was the only girl. A feeling of safety came over me. I shook my head no when they handed me a beer.

Next we are sitting at a picnic table and they told me it would cost a thousand something dollars to tow out my car. I wasn't worried because I had just received a three-thousand-dollar bill tip from a customer that was in my purse on my lap. But asked them, "Could you help me instead?" I woke up.

Interpretation

You are in charge of your life because you were driving the car which is a good thing. The car going into the water can mean a few things. Pay attention to your sobriety or you could get into deep water, but I doubt that is the meaning because your car floated instead of sinking. It can mean that you are going through an emotional clearing because water symbolizes emotions. Or you are being baptized to a new way of life. Maybe, it is a combination of all of the above?

The car floating, not sinking, and you not leaving symbolizes that you are safe and comfortable with the way things are. You don't want to let go. The edge of the water going into a fireplace means that all things must end. Also fire represents spirit which transforms things when it burns. So you will go through a spiritual shift and transformation.

The part of your dream about the house and bikers represents a bunch of things. You felt safe in a new environment and opening the door to what is coming up. The bikers represent the unknown and fear, but you are safe. You also didn't go along with the crowd and your sobriety is important to you when you – Just Say No. The fact that you had money to cover the cost shows that your needs will always be met. Lastly, it is important to ask for help and not to judge the source it comes from.

Native American Dreams

The next two dreams have Native Americans in their dreams to represent spirituality. People will use ethnicity that feels spiritual to them whether they are consciously aware of it or not. For these two women it was Native Americans. The first dream is from *In the Dreamtime* column.

<u>Dream</u>

I was hoping you could tell me the meaning of my dream. There has been a lot going on in my life and it's a dream I have never had before, it bothered me, and can't seem to shake it off.

My dream started with me, my oldest daughter, and a male figure in the kitchen. The male I felt was Native American because I saw the feathers floating around the back area of his head. This male was making pancakes. He and my daughter carried the pancakes into the dining room. I made coffee, the male came into the kitchen, and asked for my hand. He took the left hand and shoved a nail into the palm of my left hand. It didn't hurt and there was no blood, there was a hole on the top of my hand, when I turned my hand over there was a spot where he put the nail. I asked the man what that was for. He replied, "For prosperity and good luck." Then I woke up.

Interpretation

The kitchen is symbolic for the hearth of a home and where family members often meet. It makes sense that your daughter was there. I can't help but wonder if your daughter is into spirituality or you have more of a spiritual connection with her, because of what the dream reveals further along.

The Native American male feels like your guide, although it could also be that you are into Native American spirituality, or that is your heritage. However, feathers also represent angels; perhaps he is your angel? I was about to comment on the breakfast food, but my guides interrupted by saying – food for the soul. Your angel/guide is providing you with food for the soul! Pancakes are sweet with a little nutrition and fun to eat; therefore, he is also providing you with sweetness and fun to help you be healthy.

I heard, "Lend a helping hand," for the analogy of when he took your hand. The whole act of the nail in your hand is very symbolic of Jesus's resurrection. The left side of the body represents the intuitive, feminine, and the creative side of humans. Is there something along the intuitive, creative, and Goddess part of you that needs to be resurrected?

The fabulous part of this dream is the transformation you are, or will undergo, will not hurt. Your guide will be guiding you towards good luck and prosperity, so enjoy it. Trust your guide! The major symbolism about this dream is to continue down the path of spirituality and you are never alone.

The next dream was submitted to *Bellesprit Magazine* for my column; unfortunately, it was too long for the magazine.

I really love this dream and knew it would be perfect for this chapter. The dreamer was kind enough to let me use it for this book.

Dream

The dream started with me wandering around a market filled with Native Americans art, jewelry, crafts and there was a gathering of some sort going on. At first I was alone, wandering through the stalls and then there was a man. He had a Native American presence and represented by the actor Gregory Cruz (he looked like he did in the Criminal Minds episode "The Tribe." I'm including this in case it's relevant), he felt older. He was dressed in jeans and a shirt, with a brown leather jacket in the current fashion.

He handed me a beautifully crafted braided leather belt that somehow turned into a necklace of sorts, which I placed around my neck, letting it drape over my shoulders. I admired the craftsmanship and quality aloud, which made him smile. Someone else was present too, but it was him I was focused on, or rather, he was focused on me. Several times we made direct eye contact and it was as if he wanted to tell me something. I felt happy; inspired by the art and people around me (all Native American) and at peace in his company. The day was sunny and comfortable and the air filled with familiar sounds.

He stood behind me and draped a short fur cloak over my shoulders that was golden in color and fell to my waist. The cloak almost glowed in the late afternoon sun. Then he led me to a woman's house and I knew even before I arrived she was a medicine woman of sorts. It is an honor to be in her presence because she's a woman of importance.

She was dressed in traditional native clothing and had long black hair, and wearing turquoise jewelry. I had the sense she was glad I was there, as if she'd been waiting for me. She led me down a few steps into what appeared like a sun room, which was aglow with the late afternoon light. I didn't feel nervous until I saw the crows. There were two, perhaps a third, perched on a very gnarled and twisted branch on a shelf near shells and bundles of herbs.

She spoke to them, but I didn't understand what she was saying. Then she had me stand near them while she lit a bundle of sweet grass (I could smell it in my dream). She moved around me in an elegant, almost dance-like manner, surrounding me with the smoke. I closed my eyes and felt the warmth of the sun on my face and the smell of sweet grass around me. Her voice was almost sing-song in sound ... joyous. I didn't move, knowing that what she was doing was important.

Then it was quiet. When I opened my eyes, within the rays of light and smoke, I thought I saw the shimmer of glitter around her. She stood near the crows and told me to come to her. She was feeding them bits of grass and saying something to them. The crows were beautiful and I was fascinated by them, but nervous about getting too close. She insisted, taking my hand and putting the same green grass in my palm. She told me to give it to them.

I felt fear, thinking they were going to bite me. But I didn't want to disappoint her so I did as she asked. I spread my palm wide and presented the grass to them. I held my breath. To my surprise and joy, they started nibbling from my palm very gently, being almost tender and loving in their pursuit of the grass. I remember smiling and feeling a rush of warmth and joy in being accepted by them. I was laughing, then she and the man (represented by the actor Greg Cruz) were laughing and smiling too.

Whatever was happening made them happy and excited and he came to me and asked me to stay another day. I wanted to, not wanting to leave this place or the crows. In my mind, I knew I had a flight to catch, but I decided to stay. I didn't want to go. Honestly, I felt like I never wanted to go.

He took my hand and we went outside. There was music, people dancing and laughing, and the smell of something sweet and fried filling the air. I held onto his hand, afraid if I let go, this would disappear. As we walked around a tree, the late day sun nearly blinded me, and I lifted my hand to shield my eyes. And then I woke up.

To say I was devastated is an understatement. I wanted to go back. I even tried to go back to sleep to get there (I've been able to do that at other times). But unfortunately, I wasn't able to. Of all that happened, it was the crows and what happened with them that affected me so deeply, and the feeling of being home.

Interpretation

What a beautiful dream, thank you so much for sharing it with me! I could feel your serenity and wonder while reading your dream. Perhaps, you were visiting a past life. My gut is saying that it is more of a present spiritual dream regarding where you are today and where you are headed. The Native American man and woman could also be your guides. Let's begin with the interpretation.

The Native Americans represent spirituality that is more Earth based and your inner free, natural self. Your contentment throughout the dream shows that you are more comfortable with this type of spirituality than mainstream religion.

I wasn't sure who Gregory Cruz is, so I Googled him to see what he looked like, and it would seem your subconscious mind associates him with Native Americans. He also represented your inner male side. What I find interesting is both the belt/necklace and cloak went over your shoulders, which means two things to me. The first is you are getting gifts from Spirit to help deepen your spiritual male side. The second is you are now more open to heal and to work on your throat and heart chakra. You never used it as a belt that represents your root and sacral chakra. The gifts also represent joining the heart chakra to the upper chakra. This does not mean to ignore your other chakras, because it is important to focus and keep all chakras as balanced as possible.

The Native American medicine woman is your female and intuitive side. My guides added, "It is time to go further into your healing and spiritual practice." I love that the crows are in the dream, for they are my totems. Crow represents transformation, shape shifting, magic, and walking and speaking your truth. The medicine woman helped heal you to prepare you to go to your next stage in life.

When you fed the crows and felt scared is symbolic of your fear of the unknown and change. Or another way of putting it is you are afraid of feeding the unknown. The crows being lovingly gentle lets you know that your guides and Angels will protect you from harm as you transcend into a higher level. Your feelings of joy in the dream are showing you that your spiritual transformation will bring you much happiness and contentment.

The flight represents everyday commitment and reality. Who really wants that? Most people would rather stay with people that they connect with and that was shown by you wanting to stay in the happiness of the tribe. Alas, that is not reality in the physical plane. The sun blinding you could be showing you it was time to move on. Or it was spiritual energy coming to you. "They are both and remember that you can reach this state anytime you want. Just close your eyes and meditate," my guides added. I hope this interpretation helps to keep you motivated on your path.

In each of the dream examples the dreamer was ready to progress to a higher spiritual level. Some people went through the fear in their dreams and others felt peace in their dreams. The spiritual figures in these dreams were Goddesses, spiritual healing beings, a medicine woman, and Native Americans. A spiritual character that appears in a person's dreams depends on what the dreamer considers to be in most alignment with their religious and spiritual beliefs. Spiritual dreams give the dreamer answers like a solution dream, yet have more of a powerful awakening effect. This type of dream can aid you in making huge changes in your life.

Chapter Ten

Relationship Dreams

In my relationship business, during a session, some of my clients will ask me to help interpret a dream they had about their potential mate or partner. Whether the dream is about a current love interest, committed relationship, family member, friend, co-worker, or pet, it's always amazing how spot on their dreams are for their current situation. For the purpose of this chapter, we will focus on romantic relationships.

Relationships will have at least one of the dream types mentioned in the previous chapters; for example, the dream I had about the man in the gymnasium prior to actually meeting him was a pure precognitive dream. Of course a dream could have several of the styles described in this book. Whatever the style, these dreams will bring up strong emotions, and the truth regarding the present state of the relationship.

Relationship Denial Dream

People tend to go into denial when it comes to their love relationships. For instance, she couldn't be cheating on me, I can make him love me even if he was a womanizer, and my love will change them. Denial's job is to protect us from painful feelings and realities until we are better equipped to deal with a situation in our lives. This client's dream was one that stood out for me because it was such a no brainer for me to figure out. Here is the condensed version:

I was in the kitchen sitting at the table with my boyfriend and Mother. I looked at my left hand ring finger and there was a burned ring mark around it.

My interpretation was that although she wanted this relationship to go long term and into marriage, it would not. She needed to be careful because this dream was a warning that this man could hurt and burn her. My client's response was that I was wrong, this man loved her, and she felt he was her soul mate. I knew she was in denial about this, but I didn't bother to argue, and said, "This is what I am getting." She called me eight months later to tell me they had broken up and my dream interpretation was correct.

Present State of Relationship Dream

The following dream from a male reader for the *In the Dreamtime* column is a great example of how relationship dreams demonstrate our true feelings and thoughts about another person.

Dream

I dreamed that I had trouble locating my classroom as I walked around the school. Finally I found it. In the classroom (all the students were male like me) we were supposed to be quiet and study. I was reading my book when a strange woman came over and started kissing me, trying to get me to make out with her. I became uncomfortable and was happy no one was looking. I pushed her away and told her I was engaged to my girlfriend. When I woke up I was surprised that I remembered my dream because I never do. Do you know what it means?

Interpretation

When we dream about being in school it usually means that we have more lessons to learn whether you are going to school at the time or not. The fact that you found your classroom is symbolic for knowing where you are in life with either your work or life lessons. That is a very good thing. In the dream you were in a classroom with all men, so that means you are in a field of study that is either male oriented or logical. Men are symbolic in our dreams as logical thinking, male side, and physical strength.

The part where the woman is trying to get you to be sexual with her and you being uncomfortable with it, shows that you like order and structure in your life and not being the center of attention. Nor do you care for casual pickups; other men in the classroom may have jumped at that opportunity. Also that you are in a committed relationship, which means a lot to you. You are either engaged or thinking about it. It could also be a premonition of becoming engaged. Good luck to you!

Different Dream Styles

In the beginning of this chapter I mentioned how we can have one or more dream styles in our relationship dreams. My reader's dream from the December 2014 *In the Dreamtime* column illustrated this point beautifully.

This month's dream will demonstrate how dreams can have several different styles within it. Environment dreams occur when something happens before bedtime or while we're sleeping. In solution dreams, our denial or lack of time to deal with things in our waking hours comes out in our dreams. This style of dream will always reveal our true self and feelings regarding a circumstance. Prophetic dreams show the possibility of or written in stone future. Read on to see all these dream styles in this woman's dream.

<u>Dream</u>

Following an argument with my wife regarding her unambitious adult daughter, whom she defends, I had a very vivid dream. In it, I had had enough and was trying to leave. Every time I tried, they tried to have me institutionalized. I finally broke away and found myself outside desperately trying to collect playing cards that were scattering around and fluttering away from me. The cards depicted two nude women on them, which I assume from tarot means the lovers, as we are lesbians. Please help!!!

Interpretation

This is an interesting dream because it has your true feelings coming out, components of a solution dream, and even has a possibility of a prophetic dream. I will do my best to interpret it and it is up to you on which one feels right.

The part of you that has had enough, but when you tried to leave, they attempted to have you put into an institution could mean.

- *You feel ganged up on by them.*
- *They do not validate your feelings.*
- *They make you out to be the bad guy and that you are crazy.*
- *There is a part of you that is afraid you will go crazy without her if you end the relationship.*
- *I heard the song, "She Drives Me Crazy" by Fine Young Cannibals, so it could also mean she makes you crazy or is making you feel your reality is delusional.*

The two nude women card, aka "Lovers" cards, means partnership, although that does not always mean lovers. However, in your case it definitely does. This part of the dream can represent the following:

- *You feel the love in this relationship is going away and you are grasping at it.*
- *You desperately want this relationship to work.*
- *You are afraid if you leave this relationship, you will never find a romantic relationship again.*
- *The fact that there are many of the lovers cards could mean you never felt real love in any relationship.*

This is what I am picking up for you psychically.

Communication is the key, but so is acceptance. I'm not getting that you really want to go; however, you're not sure how to stay with your wife. I am hearing the Beatles song, "We Can Work It Out." And Stevie Nicks, "Talk to Me."

After I typed the above, I got a vision of a talking stick. It really feels like you two need to learn how to listen to each other. The other thing I am hearing is Stevie Nicks sing a song about how things don't change. That song is in regards to your wife and her daughter being stuck in their issues and it is their choice whether or not to work on their problems. I understand the difficulty of your position. But my guides are saying loud and clear, "The more you stay out of it, the better it will be for you and her relationship. Do your best not to let it bother you." For some reason I'm getting to keep your money separate so her daughter can't get to it.

Lastly, this dream could also be giving insight on what your life would be like without her. It is something to think about.

Relationship Fear Dream

Everyone has fears when it comes to relationships. We are afraid of never finding anyone, getting hurt, leaving a bad relationship, and commitment. Many people think it is only men that are terrified of commitment; women also have commitment fears. A quote of mine from my first book, *Psychic Wisdom on Love and Relationships*, sums up why we must work through the issues, "Relationships are where we humans get our greatest education."

A client of mine purchased an email dream interpretation, I thought her dream would be perfect for this chapter, and got permission to use it.

Dream

I dreamed that my bed was outside and it was going to rain. I asked my boyfriend for help. We walked over to the bed and I noticed a couple of frogs on it that jumped off. There was another frog that was clinging on to the bed with his nails. I pushed him off. Then, we arrived at his car; and I asked him if the bed would fit in there. He said "Yes," and took out his measuring tape to check.

The dream switched to us walking through grass. We needed to walk through a gate, but there was a huge dog in front of it that seemed friendly. He told me it was okay to pet it. I hesitated because I was afraid he would bite me. He went over and petted the dog. We walked through the gate.

Interpretation

Perhaps, at this point of the book you are able to interpret this dream? Her bed represents her sexuality and home. The rain is symbolic for cleansing and emotions. When she asked her boyfriend for help she was trusting him with not only her body, but her whole self. The frogs are her exes. The frog that clings on to the bed is either an ex that is clinging on to her, or she is holding on to an ex and/or issue. When she pushed the frog off the bed it represents her letting go and getting it out of the way.

The part of the dream where they are getting ready to

put the bed in the car could mean three things. First, the car represents the boyfriend's self, property, and travel through his life. The second meaning is that he is giving permission to go forward in the relationship to a deeper level. Thirdly, he is saying yes to the relationship, but he needs to carefully examine it.

In the next scene of the dream, the grass (without a path) represents they have walked through one part of the unknown of the relationship. The symbolism of the gate is they are ready to go to the next unknown part of the relationship that is deeper in commitment. Do you remember the dog symbols from chapter one? The symbols that work for this dog at the gate are unconditional love and loyalty. Her boyfriend petting the dog shows how he is there for her and will help her walk through her fear to the next part of their partnership.

Loving and working relationships bring so much joy into our lives! We need to work on our relationships like a garden; toiling the soil for a solid foundation, planting the seeds to slowly grow into a flower, daily water and weeding to maintain growth, and making adjustments when the relationship is in full bloom. Sadly, there are times when the plot of land dries up, nothing will grow, and it's time to move on. Our dreams of the nighttime can be used as maintenance in all our relationships.

Conclusion

The journey of learning the secret language of dreams is fascinating and well worth the effort. Our dreams help answer the question of who am I and what our purpose is. Precognitive dreams give us tools on how to handle situations that will occur in our future. All our relationships thrive and improve by the messages we receive in our dreams. We are blessed when our departed loved ones show up to say hello and I love you while in the dream state. When we humans learn how to analyze the messages of the nighttime we open ourselves up to manifest our greatest selves.

My wish in writing this book is to motivate you to delve deeper into interpreting your dreams and learn your own personal secret dream language. I realize that my book may only be one tool on your dream path, although I hope it's a powerful tool! What is important is for you to find what works best for you. If you think I can further assist you, please visit www.learndreaminterpretation.com and don't forget to get your free gift *How to Remember Your Dreams.*

May you have sweet dreams and lots of fun interpreting them!

Blessings,
Pamela Cummins

P.S. I would love it if you took the time to help this author out by leaving a review where you purchased your copy of this book.

About the Author

Pamela Cummins' dreams are absolutely wild: such as being shot in the head, meeting a man with two penises, talking to animals, and receiving visits from departed loved ones. With the guidance of a professional, she gained the knowledge of dream interpretation that helped her heal painful childhood issues. Now, Pamela loves interpreting her clients' and radio show listeners' fascinating dreams. She is the columnist for the monthly *In the Dreamtime* for Bellesprit Magazine. For more information, please visit www.learndreaminterpretation.com

More books by Pamela Cummins

Psychic Wisdom on Love and Relationships

Do feel like you will always be single? Are you sick of bad dates and relationships? Bored and unsatisfied in your relationship? *Psychic Wisdom on Love and Relationships* is a unique book packed with wisdom for BIG relationships.

Go inside the world of a psychic to see how the spirit world gives knowledge to transform your love life. This book will take you on the journey of self-love, boundaries, intuition, communication skills, and more.

Insights for Singles: Steps to Find Everlasting Love

Insights for Singles: Steps to Find Everlasting Love delivers insights to help readers reach their highest potential, learn to think positively, recognize red flags, how to let go of a relationship, improve communication skills, and understand how to *attract* and proceed with the "Right One." Whether you need to learn to "Keep your pants on" or "My fantasy is not reality," singles will find plenty of *potent* insight and *proven* solutions in this book.

Pamela's Love Collection (FREE eBook)

What do self-love, the *Three F's*, and "He has to be spiritual" have in common? They are all in *Pamela's Love Collection*. Love is always in the air, but often it's just out of our grasp. It is time to start grasping it whether you are single or in a relationship. You will learn how to recognize the signs of healthy love and what to do with it. This eBook consists of twelve articles, blogs, and columns by love intuitive and radio host Pamela Cummins.